THE CUISINE OF
ITALY
ALL THE RECIPES

edited by Silvana Franconeri

G GIUNTI DEMETRA

Editing and layout: Ilaria Stradiotti

Photography: Archivio Giunti/Arc-en-ciel, Verona

Illustrations: Mario Stoppele

Translation: Lexis, Firenze

The publisher declaires himself willing to pay any amounts due for photographs for which it has been impossible to determinate the source.

www.giunti.it

© 1999, 2003 Giunti Editore S.p.A.
Via Bolognese 165 – 50139 Firenze – Italy
Via Dante 4 – 20121 Milano – Italy

Reprint	Year		
7 6 5 4 3	2009	2008	2007

Printed and bounded by Giunti Industrie Grafiche S.p.A. - Prato (Italy)

INTRODUCTION

Italy…
Nation of artists, saints, sailors and… cooks.

Artists, saints and sailors are of the 'past' but great Italian cooking is very much alive.

Nowadays cooking is the true Italian art. Recipes of a thousand flavours and colours, resulting from a combination of imagination, curiosity and the richness of the earth.

Italy is a blend of sea and sun, plains and fog, high mountains and pure air, golden peaks and sun-drenched hills… harbours and mysterious islands.

Italy is a spectrum of many worlds which intermingle and interact with those passing through.

Italy is the story of rich people, of nobility, of monks and priests and of great poverty.

All this, enhanced by extra-virgin olive oil, has breathed life into Italian cooking, the cooking of the Mediterranean, the cooking of those who believe in the spiritual value of a hearty serving of pasta and beans.

Salami

Garlic

Wheat

Tuscan bread

Rice

Almond

Sole

Pizza

Balsamic vinegar

Extra-virgin olive oil

Mussels

Mozzarella chees

Tagliatelle

Eel

Gilthead

Clams

Pepper

Aubergine

Rosemary

Tomato

Orange

Eggs

Truffle

Sage

Basil

Parsley

Walnut

Capers

Chestnut

Blue cheese

Sardinian
pecorino cheese

Parmesan
cheese

Orecchiette

Olive

Raw
ham

Spaghetti

Tortellini

CONVERSION CHART

WEIGHT AND LENGTH	SYMBOL	CORRESPONDES TO	SYMBOL	
1 gram (grammo)	g	0.035 ounces	oz	(divide by 28 to find ounces)
1 hectogram (etto)	hg	3.57 ounces	oz	(divide by 0.28 to find ounces)
1 kilogram (chilogrammo)	kg	2.2 pounds	lb	(divide by 0.45 to find pounds)
1 millilitre (millilitro)	ml	0.03 fluid ounces	fl oz	(divide by 30 to find fluid ounces)
1 litre (litro)	l	2.1 pints	pt	(multiply by 2.1 to find pints)
		3.8 gallons (U.S.)	gal	(divide by 0.26 to find U.S. gallons)
		0.22 gallons (U.K.)	gal	(divide by 4.5 to find U.K. gallons)
1 centimeter (centimetro)	cm	0.4 inches	in	(multiply by 0.4 to find inches)
1 millimeter (millimetro)	mm	0.04 inches	in	(multiply by 0.04 to find inches)
1 meter (metro)	m	3.3 feet	ft	(multiply by 3.3 to find feet)

TEMPERATURE

Celsius degree (°C)	(°C x 1.8) + 32 to find Fahrenheit degree (°F)	180 °C corresponds to 356 °F
Fahrenheit degree (°F)	(°F − 32) x 555 to find Celsius degree (°C)	392 °F corresponds to 200 °C

NOTE

The quantities in the recipes
in the following pages
are for 4-6 servings.

STARTERS

GREEN ANCHOVIES

◀ *Valle d'Aosta-Piedmont* ▶

8 salted anchovies, yoke of hard-boiled egg, 1 clove of garlic, 1 sprig of parsley, 1 small bunch of basil, 1 red chilli pepper, 1 dessertspoon vinegar, extra-virgin olive oil.

Clean the salt from the anchovies, cut them in half and remove the bones. Crush the garlic and finely chop the parsley, basil, egg-yolk and chilli pepper and mix together with the vinegar and plenty of extra-virgin olive oil. Lay the anchovies on a serving dish; cover with the green sauce. Garnish with a few small leaves of basil and parsley and serve.

AUBERGINE STARTER

◀ *Calabria* ▶

4 aubergines, 4 cloves of garlic, 1 small bunch of basil, 2 dessertspoons apple vinegar, half a glass of extra-virgin olive oil, salt, toasted bread slices.

Wash the aubergines, cut into slices lengthwise, sprinkle with salt and leave to drain. Meanwhile finely chop the basil and crush the garlic and mix to a sauce with the oil, vinegar and salt. Rinse the aubergine slices, dry and grill for a few minutes on both sides. Remove from heat and mix them in a bowl with the basil sauce. Allow to rest for at least 10 hours in a cool place. Serve on slices of toasted bread.

BAGNA CAÛDA

◀ *Valle d'Aosta-Piedmont* ▶

200 g salted anchovies, 200 g garlic, 250 g extra-virgin olive oil, 40 g butter.

Using a damp tea-cloth, carefully re-move the salt from the anchovies. Remove the little bones, cut the anchovies into small pieces and place them in an earthenware dish with the crushed garlic. Cover with oil and cook, using a heat-diffuser plate, stirring continuously until the anchovies melt (keep the heat low so that the garlic does not brown). After about 30 minutes, melt the butter into the mixture and bring the pot to the table, keeping it hot on a small burner. The bagna caûda serves as a dip for vegetables cut into pieces, both raw (cardoons, green peppers, celery, endive, chicory etc.) and cooked (onions, beetroot, grilled peppers etc.)

For a lighter version, leave the garlic in a little milk for a few hours before crushing, then use it to flavour the oil but remove it before cooking the anchovies. In this version, a flaked white truffle can be added to the sauce before serving.

SAGE BISCUITS

◄ *Basilicata* ►

500 g flour, 1 teaspoon baking powder, 1 glass of milk, 1 small bunch of sage, 150 g butter, 1 teaspoon of salt.

In a bowl mix the flour with the baking powder, salt, chopped sage leaves and melted butter. Add milk a little at a time and mix well. Roll the dough out to about 1 cm thick and with a round cutter (or glass) cut out several biscuits and lay

them on a greased oven tray. Bake in a preheated oven for about 10 minutes.

BRUSCHETTA

◄ *Lazio* ►

One loaf of bread, garlic, extra-virgin olive oil, salt.

Bruschetta is eaten in nearly all the southern regions of Italy and there is much rivalry regarding its origins. Cut the bread into slices of about 1.5 cm in thickness and toast (best over a wood fire); when ready to serve, rub one side with a clove of garlic, sprinkle with salt and good olive oil. Serve hot. A tasty variation is a layer of tomato sauce, seasoned with basil, salt, pepper and oil. Fresh tomatoes can be used instead of sauce. Remove the seeds and extra water from the tomatoes and cut into cubes. Rub the sides of the toasted bread with garlic, spread with a layer of tomatoes, season and drizzle with extra-virgin olive oil.

9

PUGLIESE BRUSCHETTA

◄ *Puglia* ►

Pugliese bread, extra-virgin olive oil.
For the sauce: 50 g black, stoned olives, 1 dessertspoon capers, 2 anchovies with bones removed, 1/2 clove of garlic, vinegar, 2 dessertspoons of extra-virgin olive oil.

First make the sauce for the bruschetta. Rinse the anchovies in vinegar, chop and blend to a smooth mixture with olives, capers, garlic and oil.

Cut the bread into slices, toast and spread each slice with one or two spoonfuls of the mixture. Drizzle with extra-virgin olive oil.

To vary, cook some broccoli in simmering salt water, flavour with oil and spread on the toasted bread with the sauce.

SCALLOPS AU GRATIN

◀ *Veneto* ▶

2-3 scallops for each guest, breadcrumbs, 1 sprig of parsley, cognac, butter, salt, freshly ground pepper.

Clean the scallops by discarding the flat part of the shell and detaching the shellfish. Mix a few spoonfuls of breadcrumbs with the chopped parsley, a pinch of salt, some freshly ground pepper and a drop of cognac (the mixture should not be too soft).

Roll the shellfish in the breadcrumbs, place them back in the shells, add a drop of cognac and a small lump of butter. Cook the scallops in a hot oven for about ten minutes and serve hot.

CAZZILLI

◀ *Sicily* ▶

1 kg potatoes, 1 clove of garlic, 1 sprig of parsley, 2 beaten egg-whites, breadcrumbs, olive oil, salt, pepper.

Boil the potatoes in their jackets. Peel and mash them, add the crushed garlic and parsley and flavour with salt and pepper.

Roll the cooled mixture into oval shapes and dip them first into the beaten egg white, then the breadcrumbs and fry in very hot oil. Drain and allow to dry on absorbent kitchen paper, dust with salt and serve while hot.

CECINA

◀ *Tuscany* ▶

500 g chickpea meal, 1 glass of extra-virgin olive oil, salt, freshly ground black pepper.

Steep the chickpea meal in 2 litres of water then stir with a wooden spoon. Add the oil and a pinch of salt, then pour the mixture into a wide oven tray with low sides. Bear in mind that the cecina should not be over 5mm thick: if you do not have a wide oven tray, use two smaller trays.

Cook in a hot oven until a golden crust has formed. Cut into pieces and dust with freshly ground black pepper.

STUFFED MUSSELS

◀ *Marche* ▶

1 kg mussels, 300 g ripe, firm tomatoes, 1 sprig

of parsley, 1 clove of garlic, breadcrumbs, extra-virgin olive oil, salt, pepper.

Scrape the mussels (or muscoli as they are called in the Marche) under running water and allow them to open in a pot over a rapid heat; as they open discard the empty half and place the part containing the mussel on an oven tray.

Plunge the tomatoes into boiling water so they can be skinned easily, remove their seeds and chop them. Mix the tomatoes with finely chopped parsley and garlic, salt, freshly ground pepper, oil and a few spoonfuls of bread-crumbs to give a soft, yet firm consistency. Place the filling on the mussels and drizzle with oil. Allow to cook in a preheated oven for about ten minutes. To vary the recipe add approximately 50 grams of roughly chopped Parma ham to the filling mixture.

CRESCIA

◀ Marche ▶

1 kg maize flour, 200 g flour, 1 kg pork loin, 400 g chard, 400 g cabbage, 400 g chicory, 100 g lard, 2 cloves of garlic, white wine, extra-virgin olive oil, salt, pepper.

Dice the pork loin and cook in a little oil over a rapid heat for an hour, frequently adding white wine. Season. In the meantime clean the vegetables and boil in a little salt water. When cooked, fry the vegetables in the pan with the chopped lard, cloves of garlic and a pinch of pepper.

Prepare the crescia, which is a tradi-tional type of pizza from the city of Fabriano. In a large bowl mix together the two types of flour with a pinch of salt and hot water to make a soft dough. Place the mixture into a deep-sided baking dish and cook in a pre-heated oven (250° C) for about an hour. When the crescia is ready it will have a hard crust but be soft inside. Cut into large squares, halve, fill with meat and vegetables and serve immediately. This is a very substantial dish which is suitable for a winter meal. Instead of the above vegetables, you can use any at hand. Butter or oil can be used instead of lard.

CROSTINI WITH TRUFFLES

◀ Umbria ▶

Toasted bread slices, black truffle to taste, anchovy fillets, 1 lemon, extra-virgin oil

Carefully clean and wash the truffle and grate a little to flavour the crostini (a lot depends on the quality of the truffle). Heat a little oil in a metal pan and add the grated truffle. After a few moments add the

chopped anchovy fillets and the lemon juice and mix carefully. Spread the prepared mixture on the toasted bread and serve.

CROSTINI ALLA CIOCIARA

◄ Lazio ►

Bread slices, fresh caprino, (goat's milk cheese), ripe, firm tomatoes, black olives, vinegar, extra-virgin olive oil, chilli powder.

Heat the chopped caprino with the oil and vinegar in a small pan over a low heat. Stir and allow the cheese to melt. Cut the tomatoes into cubes, remove the stones from the olives, slice and add to the mixture with a pinch of chilli powder. Allow to cook for a few minutes while you toast the bread. Arrange the toast on a plate and spread with the mixture.

CROSTINI WITH "LIPTAUER"

◄ Friuli Venezia Giulia ►

250 g ricotta, 100 g butter, 1 dessertspoon capers, 1 small teaspoon sweet paprika, 1 dessertspoon mustard, 1 sprig of parsley, a few spring onions, salt, pepper.

In a bowl beat the ricotta with a fork or egg beater and add the other ingredients one at a time: the butter, first softened and cut into pieces, the rinsed and chopped capers, then the paprika, mustard, chopped parsley and spring onion. Mix to obtain a soft cream. Place in the fridge to allow the flavours to blend. Serve with slices of rye bread.

CROSTINI WITH CHICKEN LIVERS

◄ Tuscany ►

250 g chicken livers, 1 small onion, 3 anchovies, 1 dessertspoon capers, butter, white wine, bread slices, salt, freshly ground pepper.

Cook the sliced onion in the butter, add the cleaned livers and a little white wine. Add salt. When the sauce thickens, remove from heat and mash the livers together with the anchovies and capers. Cook together for a few more minutes with a little butter and some freshly ground pepper and spread the mixture on a few slices of toasted bread.

ERBAZZONE

◄ Emilia Romagna ►

1 kg spinach, 100 g flour, 60 g lard, 100 g bacon, 1 small onion, 1 clove of garlic, 300 g breadcrumbs, 200 g Parmesan cheese, 4 eggs, salt, pepper.

Wash the spinach carefully, cook in boiling water, drain and squeeze out excess water. Chop finely. Meanwhile prepare the dough with the flour, lard, water and salt. Form a ball and leave to chill in the fridge for half an hour.
Clean and chop the onion and garlic and cook together with the bacon. Add the cooked spinach and cook together for a few minutes. Remove from heat, add the breadcrumbs, cheese, eggs and salt.
Remove the dough from the fridge, divide into two halves and roll out two

13

sheets about 1 cm thick. Grease a pie dish and cover the bottom with one of the pastry sheets. Place the filling on top and cover with the remaining sheet.

Prick the surface with a fork and cook at a low heat (160°) for about half an hour. Serve hot or cold.

FETTUNTA

◀ Tuscany ▶

4 slices of stale bread, 2 cloves of garlic, extra-virgin oil, salt, freshly ground pepper.

This is a very simple recipe which owes its success mainly to the quality of the oil (the ideal is cold pressed oil). Toast the bread, which must be at least a day old, on embers (or oven grill). When crisp, rub with a clove of garlic, sprinkle with salt and some good freshly ground black pepper.

Drizzle oil over the slices and serve im-

14

mediately while still hot, before the oil has soaked completely into the bread.

FIADONE

◀ Abruzzo-Molise ▶

<u>For the pastry</u>: *300 g flour, 3 eggs, 1 teaspoon baking powder, 1/2 glass of milk, 2 dessertspoons oil, salt, pepper.*
<u>For the filling</u>: *500 g of pecorino or goat's cheese, grated, (or half Parmesan cheese and half pecorino), 4 eggs, 1 teaspoon baking powder, nutmeg, freshly ground pepper.*

This is a country pie which is typical of the Easter period. Start by preparing the pastry: mix the flour with a pinch each of salt and pepper and make a well on your work surface. Break two eggs into the well and pour in the oil. Dissolve the baking powder in the milk and pour into the well. Knead into a dough, roll out and line a pie dish. Allow the pastry to overlap the edges.

Leave a little dough aside for decoration.

To prepare the filling, beat the eggs and add plenty of freshly ground pepper and a pinch of nutmeg. Mix the grated cheese with the baking powder and add to the egg mixture. Mix together to allow the ingredients to swell.

Cover the pastry with the mixture and turn over the borders. Decorate the surface with the remaining pastry. Brush some egg yolk over the pie and cook in a moderate oven for about 45 minutes, or until the fiadone is golden.

CRAB WITH LEMON

◀ *Veneto* ▶

1 crab, not too large, for each guest, 1 lemon, parsley, extra-virgin olive oil, salt pepper.

Boil the crabs in plentiful salt water (possibly flavoured with onion, bay leaves and parsley). After 30 minutes, remove them from the water and allow them to cool. Detach the backs from the legs.

Extract the pulp from the shells and the legs, chop and replace in the shells which have been carefully cleaned. Drizzle with oil and lemon juice and season with salt and pepper. Serve garnished with chopped parsley.

SEAFOOD SALAD

◀ *Campania* ▶

3 kg shellfish (mussels, clams, razor clams), 6 ba-

by squid, 1-2 lemons, 3 cloves of garlic, 1 sprig of parsley, 1 bay leaf, salt, freshly ground pepper.*

Clean the baby squid; if they are small leave them whole, otherwise separate the tentacles from the sac and cut the latter into 3-4 pieces. Drop into boiling salt water with a few slices of lemon, the bay leaves and some pepper corns; let them boil for three or four minutes and drain well. Clean the mussels and clams and allow them to open in a pan with a few spoonfuls of oil and some crushed garlic. Once open, remove from the heat, remove the shells and filter the liquid in the pan.

Place the shellfish and the baby squid in a serving dish and flavour them with the filtered cooking oil flavoured with lemon, pepper and chopped parsley. The salad is tastier if served lukewarm.

NERVETTI

◀ *Lombardy* ▶

2 calves' feet, 1/2 calf's head, 2 veal fillets, 4 large fresh onions, 1 carrot, 1 stalk of celery, 1 small bunch of parsley, 1-2 dessertspoons of vinegar, 5 dessertspoons of extra virgin olive oil, salt, pepper.

Clean the pieces of meat. Rinse under running water and leave to dry well.

In a large pot make a stock with plentiful water, celery and carrot, then add the meat and leave to simmer slowly for about 2 hours. Remove the meat from the stock and when lukewarm, remove the bones carefully.

Cut the meat into small strips and place together in a large dish. Add the thinly sliced fresh onions, some chopped parsley, a pinch of salt and pepper and the oil and vinegar. Stir well to allow the flavours to blend and serve.

MOZZARELLA IN CARROZZA

◀ Campania ▶ 📷

8 slices of stale bread, 1 large mozzarella, 2 eggs, anchovies in oil (optional), white flour, milk, olive oil, salt, pepper.

Cut the mozzarella in quite thick slices and place each slice between two slices of bread. To vary the flavour, if you wish, you can add an anchovy fillet with the salt and bones removed. Press the whole together and dip it first into the flour then into the beaten egg to which has been added some milk, salt and pepper. When the bread is fairly moist, brown on both sides in hot oil. Drain the mozzarella in carozza and leave to dry on absorbent kitchen paper. Serve while still hot.

OLIVE ALL'ASCOLANA

◀ Marche ▶

1 kg large green olives, 150 g minced veal, 150 g chopped pork, 100 g Parma ham, chopped, 100 g grated pecorino, 100 g grated Parmesan, 2 dessertspoons tomato pulp, 4 eggs, nutmeg, breadcrumbs, white wine, extra-virgin olive oil, salt, pepper.

Brown the meat in a pan with a little oil, salt and pepper. Add a little white wine and as soon as it has evaporated cover the saucepan and remove from heat. In a bowl mix the cooked meat, the chopped Parma ham, the cheese, breadcrumbs, a pinch of nutmeg, the tomato pulp and two eggs. Mix well to a soft paste. Remove the stones from the olives and fill them with the mixture. Dip them into the remaining beaten egg and roll them in breadcrumbs. Fry in hot oil and serve hot.

DRESSED OLIVES

◀ Puglia ▶

Large black olives, 1 whole chilli pepper, chilli powder, garlic, parsley, extra-virgin olive oil.

Make a small cut on the olives and place them in a marinade of oil, chopped pepper, chilli powder, sliced or crushed garlic. Leave for 24 hours, shaking from time to time.
The olives can be served immediately, or a few days later, sprinkled with some chopped parsley.

16

FRIED OLIVES

◀ *Sicily* ▶

40 large black olives, 2 cloves of garlic, oregano, 1 small glass of vinegar, extra-virgin olive oil.

Crush the garlic and cook for a few minutes in oil. Add the olives and vinegar and continue to cook until the liquid is reduced. Add oregano. Serve very hot.

PANZANELLA

◀ *Tuscany* ▶

400 g stale bread, 3 ripe tomatoes, 1 red onion, 1 cucumber, 6 basil leaves, 1 teaspoon vinegar, 3 dessertspoons of extra-virgin olive oil, salt, pepper.

This is a country dish which was traditionally eaten for breakfast or a snack. It can be served as a starter or first course.
Steep the bread in water to soften. Meanwhile, peel and slice the cucumber and sprinkle with salt. Squeeze between two plates to remove excess water.
Finely slice the onion and tomatoes and tear the basil leaves into small pieces.
Squeeze the moisture from the bread and crumble it in a bowl, add the cucumber which has been rinsed free of salt, the onion and tomatoes. Flavour with vinegar, oil, salt and freshly ground pepper. Mix lightly and leave to rest in a cool place for 10 minutes before serving.

An older version of the recipe does without the cucumber, while other variations use celery, garlic or wild herbs such as rocket.

TOMATO *PANZEROTTI*

◀ *Puglia* ▶

<u>For the pastry</u>: *400 g white flour, 25 g fresh yeast, 50 g extra-virgin olive oil, salt.*
<u>For the filling</u>: *250 g mozzarella, 400 g small ripe tomatoes, oregano, extra-virgin olive oil, olive oil for frying, salt, red chilli pepper.*

Make a well of the flour on the work surface. Crumble the yeast in the centre of the well and dissolve it in a spoonful of lukewarm water. Add salt, oil and enough water to make a manageable dough. Knead the dough until it becomes soft and elastic. Make a ball, roll it in flour and cover with a clean teacloth, leaving it to rise in a warm place for about two and a half hours.
Meanwhile prepare the filling. Skin the tomatoes by plunging them in boiling water, remove the seeds, chop them and cook them in a little extra-virgin olive oil until they thicken. Add oregano, chilli powder and salt and remove from heat.
Knead the dough again for a few minutes and divide into 8 or 10 pieces, flattening each into a thin disk. At the centre of every disk place a cube of mozzarella, a little tomato sauce, add a little more chilli and oregano and fold over into a half-moon shape, pressing the moistened edges together to seal.
Fry the panzerotti in hot oil, turning

them so they become golden all over; drain and leave to dry on kitchen paper. Serve hot.

on a moderate heat, stirring now and again. Before serving, add salt and some freshly ground pepper to taste.

RED CHICORY IN *SAÓR*

◀ *Veneto* ▶

8 heads of red chicory, 150 g onion, 40 g raisins, 30 g pine-nuts, 1/2 glass red wine vinegar, 3 dessertspoons extra-virgin olive oil, 1 teaspoon sugar, salt, freshly ground pepper.

Wash the chicory heads, dry in a salad spinner and cut into four pieces lengthways. Leave the raisins to steep in a little lukewarm water for an hour. Peel and finely slice the onions, cook them for a few minutes in oil, stirring with a wooden spoon. While stirring, add the vinegar and the pine-nuts. Allow some of the liquid to evaporate and add the chicory, continue cooking

SALAMI IN VINEGAR

◀ *Friuli Venezia Giulia* ▶

8 large slice of fresh salami, 1/2 onion, 2 dessertspoons of red wine vinegar, 50 g butter.

Soften the onion in butter, add the salami slices and brown on either side, add vinegar and allow the liquid to evaporate.
Serve the salami hot, accompanied by small slices of grilled polenta.

RICE CROQUETTES

◀ *Lazio* ▶

19

250 g rice, 50 g grated Parmesan, 3 eggs, flour,

PILCHARDS IN *SAOR*

◀ *Veneto* ▶ 📷

700 g fresh pilchards, 700 g onions, 1 lemon, 1 handful raisins, 4 bay leaves, 3 cloves, white flour, 2 glasses of vinegar, extra-virgin olive oil, salt, pepper.

◆ Soften the raisins in lukewarm water. Clean the pilchards by removing the bones and discarding the heads. Wash and leave to dry on a tea-cloth. When dry, roll them in flour and fry them in hot oil; leave to dry on kitchen paper. In the same oil, cook the onions cut into thin rings, add two glasses of vinegar and the grated lemon peel. Cook for a minute or two, then remove from heat.

◆ In glass jars, place a layer of fried fish, salt and pepper, and cover with a layer of onions, cloves, bay leaves and raisins. Continue alternating the ingredients until there are none left, finishing with the onions. Cover and keep in the fridge a few days before serving. As well as raisins, pine nuts or small apple slices can be used. Saór or "flavour" – one of the tastiest preserving methods typical of the Veneto province – is suitable for nearly all types of fish, from small fish to sole.

20

breadcrumbs, 1 litre stock, 50 g butter, olive oil, salt, pepper.

For the filling: 1 mozzarella, 1 slice of Parma ham (about 100 g), 50 g tomato sauce, 2 spoonfuls of grated Parmesan, 1 sprig of parsley, pepper.

With the knob of butter, the rice and hot stock make a risotto. Season to taste and flavour with a sprinkling of nutmeg. Remove the rice from the heat when it is still al dente, add the grated cheese and allow to cool spread out on a serving dish.

In the meantime prepare the filling: in a bowl mix the mozzarella and the ham cut into cubes together with the tomato sauce, grated cheese, chopped parsley and plenty of freshly ground pepper. With wet hands, take some rice and roll into oval balls. Stuff the balls with the mozzarella filling and close. Dip the balls into the beaten egg and the breadcrumbs. Brown them evenly in hot oil, drain and leave to dry on absorbent kitchen paper.

Serve hot after sprinkling with salt.

In another version, the rice croquettes are stuffed with meat sauce prepared with minced veal and sweetbreads.

They can be prepared with risotto (of tomato or mushrooms etc.) left over from the day before.

SWEET-SAVOURY PIE

◀ Basilicata ▶

300 g white flour, 150 g sugar, 150 g butter, 2 egg yolks, salt

For the filling: 350 g fresh ricotta, 100 g cheese, 1 mozzarella, 30 g grated pecorino, 2 slices Parma ham (approx. 50 g each), 2 egg yolks, 1 egg, 25 g sugar, extra-virgin oil, salt, pepper.

Mix the flour with the sugar and a pinch of salt, make a well in the centre and drop in the softened butter which has been cut into little pieces and 2 egg yolks. Work the ingredients together to obtain a soft, smooth dough. Leave to rest, covered, in a cool place for about one hour.

In the meantime prepare the filling. In a bowl beat the ricotta with a fork and add the other ingredients one at a time: the crumbled cheese, the ham and mozzarella cut into pieces, the egg and 2 yolks, salt and some freshly ground pepper. Mix well: the mixture should be soft in consistency.

Divide the dough into two portions and roll out into round sheets only a few millimetres thick with a floured rolling pin. Line the bottom and sides of a greased pie dish with one sheet. Spread the filling on top, cover with the smaller

21

circle and seal the edges well, pressing into a braid. Brush the surface with beaten egg yolk and cook in a moderate oven (160°C) for about one hour.

Pasqualina (easter) pie

◀ Liguria ▶

For the pastry: 600 g flour, 2 dessertspoons of extra-virgin olive oil, salt.
For the filling: 8 artichokes, 200 g herbs, 400 g ricotta, 100 g butter, 10 eggs, 50 g grated Parmesan cheese, 1 clove of garlic, parsley, marjoram, 1 lemon, 2 dessertspoons flour, salt.

Discard the hard outer leaves, stalks and thorns of the artichokes, cut them lengthways into slices and steep them in water and lemon juice. Sieve the flour onto the table and make a well. In the centre pour the oil, 1/2 litre lukewarm water and the salt and knead for 15 minutes to obtain a soft dough. Cover with a dry cloth with a damp one on top and allow to rest.
Wash the herbs, cook them in a little water, strain, squeeze well and chop. In a pot cook the clove of garlic in 50 g butter, add the drained artichokes, cover them and let them cook slowly. When they are nearly cooked add a little chopped parsley. Remove the artichokes from the pot and mix the herbs into the cooking liquid.
In a bowl mix the ricotta, the grated Parmesan, 3 eggs, flour, salt and pepper, add the cooled herbs and artichokes but discard the garlic.
Divide the dough into ten pieces. Keeping the others covered to prevent them from drying, roll out four pieces thinly (one at a time). Place these sheets one on top of the other in a round cake tin, brushing the first three with oil. Allow the pastry to stick to the bottom and sides, leaving about 1 cm of pastry overlapping the top. Place the filling in the centre. With the back of a spoon make seven hollows and break an egg into each, add a teaspoon of melted butter and one of Parmesan cheese, salt and pepper. Take the other pieces of dough, roll out and cover the filling, using the same procedure and brushing each with oil. Cut away the overlapping pastry all around the cake pan and shape a wide braid to place around the edge. Brush the last sheet with oil and prick the pastry with a fork, being careful not to break the eggs. Bake the pie in a moderate oven for about one hour until the surface has become golden brown. Serve hot.

VOL-AU-VENT MUSHROOMS

◀ *Valle d'Aosta-Piedmont* ▶ 📷

4 vol-au-vents, 10 champignon mushrooms, 50 g taleggio cheese, 20 g butter, paprika, salt, freshly ground black pepper.

◆ Brown the sliced mushrooms in butter for about 10 minutes and season with salt and pepper.

◆ In a bowl, mix the cheese with the freshly ground black pepper, salt, a pinch of paprika and the mushroom gravy.

◆ Fill the vol-au-vents with the cream, garnish with mushrooms and place in a preheated oven to warm.

FOCACCIA, BREAD, PIZZA, SAVOURY PIES

CALZONE

◀ *Campania* ▶

<u>For the pastry</u>: 350 g white flour, 25 g fresh brewers yeast, butter.
<u>For the filling</u>: 200 g mozzarella, 100 g salami, 100 g cooked ham, 100 g fresh ricotta, 1 egg, 4 dessertspoons grated pecorino, 6-8 dessertspoons of extra-virgin olive oil, salt, pepper.

Start by making a well of the flour on the work surface. Crumble the yeast in the centre, dissolve in a dessertspoon of lukewarm water, add the salt, a knob of butter and enough water to knead the mixture into a soft, smooth dough. Leave the dough to rise in a warm place, protected from draughts.
When the dough has risen, roll it out on a floured pastry board or a suitable work surface, to obtain four rounds which are not too thin. Allow to rest for about twenty minutes on the oven tray or in a pan.
Cut the mozzarella, salami and the ham into small cubes, mix with the beaten egg and the grated cheese, salt and pepper to taste. Finally add the crumbled ricotta. Divide this mixture between the four rounds and fold each one into a half-moon shape. Press the edges together and bake in a very hot oven for about a quarter of an hour.

CALZONE WITH VEGETABLES

◀ *Basilicata* ▶

300 g bread dough, 1 kg chard, 75 g black olives, extra-virgin olive oil, salt, chilli powder.

Wash the chard, dry thoroughly and cut into small strips. In a bowl mix the chard with the stoned and chopped olives, oil, salt and a pinch of chilli powder. Divide the dough into small portions and roll out on the floured working surface to an oval shape. In the centre of each portion drop some of the chard filling, fold over and seal the edges with a little water.
Place the calzoni on some greaseproof paper on an oven tray. Cook in a preheated oven (180° C) for about 20-30 minutes.

CRESCENTA

◀ *Emilia Romagna* ▶

500 g flour, 50 g fresh yeast, 50g. lard, 1 dessertspoon extra-virgin olive oil, salt.

The batter can be obtained by using water or 1/2 glass of milk instead of the oil. In a large bowl or on a work surface mix the flour, the oil, crumbled brewers yeast and some salt. Knead to obtain a consistent dough and allow to rise covered by a clean tea-cloth.

After about half an hour roll out the dough to obtain a sheet of pastry about two centimetres thick. Cut into diamond shapes about 8cm in length.

Melt the lard in a wide frying pan over a lively flame. When it starts to bubble fry the pastry diamonds until they turn golden and swell. Turn them over delicately using a spatula and lay them on absorbent kitchen paper to drain away excess oil.

Serve the crescenta very hot accompanied by salami, cold pork and flakes of Parmesan cheese.

FOCACCIA WITH OIL

◀ *Liguria* ▶

500 g flour, 30 g fresh yeast, 1 dl extra-virgin olive oil, salt.

Dissolve the yeast in a cup of lukewarm water, add to the flour and knead well to obtain a soft dough. Cover with a tea-cloth and leave to rest for about 2 hours in a warm environment. Once risen, roll out the dough to not more than 2 centimetres thick. Place the dough on a baking sheet which has been previously greased and sprinkled with salt. Pinch the surface of the focaccia with your fingers, sprinkle with a little more salt and drizzle with oil. Cook in a hot oven for about twenty minutes. Serve the focaccia hot or cold.

There are many variations including the following: before putting the focaccia into the oven, sprinkle the surface with rosemary.

CARASAU BREAD OR "MUSIC SHEET" BREAD

◀ *Sardinia* ▶ 📷

1 kg durum wheat flour, 10 g fresh yeast, 1 dessertspoon coarse salt.

Dissolve the yeast in a little lukewarm water and the salt separately in less than 5dl lukewarm water. Add the yeast to the flour and then knead with some salt water to obtain a soft, damp, smooth dough. Shape some balls about 8cm in diameter and

30

leave to rise for about four hours in a dry place. Roll out the dough, keeping it constantly floured so it does not stick, to obtain circles of about 2-3 mm thick and 40cm in diameter. Cook the sheets of pastry one on top of the other in a very hot oven and separate them when they begin to swell. At this point the bread is called "lentu". To make carasau bread replace it in the oven until it is dry and crunchy.

FRATTAU BREAD

◀ *Sardinia* ▶

Several slices of "music sheet" bread, tomato sauce, minced meat, eggs, 1 onion, 1 clove of garlic, grated pecorino, extra-virgin olive oil, salt.

Make a meat sauce by cooking the onion in oil, browning the minced meat, and adding the tomato sauce. Put the "music sheets" one at a time in plenty of boiling salt water for a few seconds, remove and lay out on serving dishes. Cover each with the meat sauce. Flavour with grated pecorino and add a poached egg to each serving.

PUGLIESE BREAD

◀ *Puglia* ▶ 📷

2 kg flour, 40 g dry or fresh yeast, 10 g malt, 40 g salt.

Dissolve the yeast in a little lukewarm water, then knead all the ingredients

together with 1.5 litres of water for about 20 minutes to obtain a soft smooth dough. Cover and allow to rest for about 2 hours, then knead again and divide into loaves. Leave again, with the closing seam of the dough facing upwards. After half an hour, flatten and overturn the loaves and leave to rest for a further 30 minutes. With the point of a knife make a circular cut on the surface of the bread and bake it in a hot oven (220°C) for about 40 minutes.

TUSCAN BREAD

◀ *Tuscany* ▶

1.4 kg fine white flour, 60 g fresh yeast.

The typical Tuscan bread is "sciocco", i.e. without salt, a tradition that has spread to the regions of Umbria and upper Lazio, the areas occupied by the ancient Etruscans.
Knead the flour with baking powder and water and leave to rise for a few hours.
Once risen, shape the dough into loaves, either a large loaf or a French loaf to weigh about 500g once baked.

Make cross cuts on the surface and bake in a hot oven (about 210-220°C). The baked bread should have a crispy crust and a honeycomb texture inside. It is the best bread for preparing bruschette, crostini and fettunte.

PIADINA ROMAGNOLA

◀ *Emilia Romagna* ▶

500 g flour, 150 g lard, 1 teaspoon salt.

Mix the flour, salt and lard with enough water to obtain a smooth dough. Knead for 10 minutes and divide the mixture into several pieces the size of an egg. Roll these out to form thin rounds.
As you prepare the piadine, lay them one over the other. Dust with flour and cover with a cloth. Heat an iron-based pot (the traditional method uses a firebrick) and cook the piadine on both sides, pricking them with a fork. Place them one on top of the other and cover with a cloth to keep warm.
Eat with a filling of Parma ham or cheese or serve as a side dish.

POTATO PIZZA

◀ *Puglia* ▶

200 g potatoes, 100 g flour, 250 g ripe, firm tomatoes, 2 salted anchovies, 100 g black olives, 1 dessertspoon salted capers, oregano, extra-virgin olive oil, salt, chilli powder.

Boil potatoes in salt water, peel and mash them and turn them over onto a

floured
pastry board.
Add flour, a pinch of salt and knead to obtain a soft, smooth dough. Grease a pizza tray with oil and line it with the potato pastry. Peel tomatoes, remove seeds and chop and spread over the potato pastry. Remove the salt from the anchovies and lay on the tomatoes, Add the olives, with their stones removed, and washed and dried capers. Season with salt, chilli powder, oregano and a dash of oil, and cook in a hot oven (180°) for about 30 minutes.

CHICORY PIZZA

◀ Campania ▶

For the pastry: 400 g flour, 25 g fresh yeast, 50 g extra-virgin olive oil, salt.
For the filling: 800 g chicory, 2 cloves of garlic, 2 dessertspoons salted capers, 1 dessertspoon raisins, 20 black olives with stones removed, extra-virgin olive oil, salt, chilli powder.

Form a well with the flour on a work surface. Crumble the yeast in the centre and dissolve it in a spoonful of lukewarm water, add salt, oil and sufficient water to make a smooth, soft dough.

Knead the dough until it becomes soft and elastic. Form a ball of the dough, dust with flour and cover with a damp cloth, leaving to rise in a warm place shielded from draughts, for about two and a half hours.

Meanwhile prepare the chicory: wash and steam, then fry in a pan with some oil and the cloves of garlic. Season with salt and chilli powder just before removing from the heat.

When the dough has risen adequately, flatten on a pastry board and divide into two equal portions. Grease an oven tray and line with one portion of the dough. Mix the chicory with rinsed capers, olives, and raisins which have been steeped in a little warm water. Spread filling over the pastry base and cover with the remaining dough. Cook in the oven for about 40 minutes. Serve hot or cold..

NEAPOLITAN PIZZA

◀ Campania ▶

For the pastry: 400 g flour, 25 g fresh yeast, 50 g extra-virgin olive oil, salt.
For flavouring: 400 g peeled tomatoes, 3 cloves of garlic, a few leaves of basil or oregano, extra-virgin olive oil, salt.

Form a well with the flour. Crumble the yeast in the centre of the well and dissolve in a spoonful of lukewarm water. Add the salt, oil and sufficient water to knead. Knead until the dough becomes soft and elastic. Form a ball with the dough, dust with flour and

33

Form a well with the flour on a pastry table or suitable work surface. Crumble the yeast into the centre and dissolve in a spoonful of lukewarm water, add the salt, the oil and sufficient water to obtain a smooth, soft and manageable dough.

Knead the dough vigorously until it becomes soft and elastic. Form a ball of the dough, cover with a damp tea-cloth and leave it to rise in a warm place, protected from draughts, for about two and a half hours.

Roll the risen dough with a rolling pin to a rectangular or round shape according to the oven tray you want to use. Lay the dough on the greased pizza tray, or directly onto the oven tray, spread with the tomato sauce, prick lightly with a fork and leave to rest again in a warm place for a further 20 minutes or so.

Place in a hot oven (200-250°) for about 20 minutes. Remove from the oven, spread the finely sliced raw onions over the pizza with the rosemary and drizzle with oil. Replace in oven for a further 20 minutes.

The pizza can be served with slices of salted Parma ham.

cover with a damp cloth. Leave to rise in a warm place for about two and a half hours protected from draughts.

Once the dough has risen, roll out on a floured surface to a round or a rectangular sheet. Cover with the peeled tomatoes, which have been mashed with a fork, prick the surface slightly, sprinkle with salt and leave to rest for about twenty minutes. Cook in a hot oven (200-250°) for about 20 minutes. Remove from the oven and season with a pinch of oregano or chopped basil and crushed garlic, drizzle with oil and replace in the oven for five more minutes prior to serving.

COUNTRY PIZZA WITH ONION

◀ Umbria ▶

For the pastry: 400 g flour, 25 g fresh yeast, 50 g of extra-virgin olive oil, salt.
For flavouring: tomato sauce, 3 onions, rosemary, extra-virgin olive oil, salt.

dough on a greased oven tray, cover with the sliced onions, slices of cacio-cavallo and the tomato sauce and bake in a hot oven for 15 minutes.

TARALLUCCI

◀ Calabria ▶

300 g flour, 2 eggs, 2 dessertspoons dry, white wine, 2 dessertspoons extra-virgin olive oil, salt, chilli powder.

Mix the flour with the eggs, oil, white wine and a pinch each of chilli powder and salt. Divide and shape the dough into small "pleats" of about 10cm in length and form circles by joining the ends. In a pot boil some salt water and drop in the tarallucci. As soon as they float to the top remove them with a slotted spoon and lay them on a greased oven tray. Cook in a hot oven (180°) for about twenty minutes. The tarallucci can be varied by substituting the chilli powder with fennel seeds or adding a spoonful of olive sauce and a few chopped olives to the mixture.

35

SFINCIUNI

◀ Sicily ▶

600 g leavened bread dough, 6 slices of fresh ca-ciocavallo (gourd-shaped cheese from southern Italy), 4 anchovy fillets, 6 tomatoes, 3 onions, 1 clove of garlic, 1 basil leaf, 1 dessertspoon of breadcrumbs, extra-virgin olive oil, salt, pepper.

Cook the garlic clove in the oil, add peeled and chopped tomatoes, basil leaves and the anchovy fillets, crushing them until they break up. Add salt and pepper and the breadcrumbs. Lay the

SAUCES

MEAT SAUCE WITH AROMATIC VINEGAR

◀ *Emilia Romagna* ▶

400 g boned veal, 100 g bacon, 1 handful of dried mushrooms, 3 skinned tomatoes, 2 stalks celery, 1 onion, 1 carrot, 2 bay leaves, 1 pinch powdered cinnamon, 50 g butter, 2 dessertspoons aromatic vinegar, salt, freshly ground pepper.

Wash the mushrooms and leave to steep in some lukewarm water. Clean and chop the celery, onion and carrot. Heat butter in a pan and cook the chopped vegetables, stirring with a wooden spoon. Meanwhile cut the boned veal into small pieces. When the vegetable mixture has browned, add the tomatoes, crushing them with a fork, and then add the meat and leave to cook on a low heat for a few minutes. Add the strained mushrooms, cinnamon and the bay leaves. Season with salt, freshly ground pepper and vinegar and cook for an hour on a moderate heat, stirring from time to time.

SEA URCHIN SAUCE

◀ *Sardinia* ▶

30 sea urchins, 400 g ripe tomatoes, 1 onion, 2 cloves of garlic, parsley, saffron, extra-virgin olive oil, salt, pepper.

Clean the sea urchins by extracting the inner part with a teaspoon. Peel the tomatoes, remove the seeds and chop into large pieces. Dissolve some saffron, salt and pepper in hot water or fish or vegetable stock. Cook the chopped onion in plenty of oil. Add tomatoes to the onion with a ladle of seasoned hot water or stock. Continue cooking for 15 minutes on a low heat, then add the urchin pulp and some chopped garlic and parsley. Turn off heat when the tomato is cooked. If necessary add some more hot water or stock to prevent the sauce drying out.

SORRENTINA SAUCE

◀ *Campania* ▶

300 g firm, ripe tomatoes, 1 sprig of parsley, a few basil leaves, 1/2 lemon, extra-virgin olive oil, salt, pepper.

Plunge the tomatoes into boiling water so they can be peeled easily, then remove the seeds and chop them or cut into thin slices. In a bowl, flavour the tomatoes with the lemon juice, salt, freshly ground pepper, some finely chopped parsley, a few finely chopped basil leaves and a dash of oil. Cover the container and let it rest in a cool place to allow the flavours to blend. Use the sauce for flavouring spaghetti or gnocchi.

PEARÀ SAUCE
◀ *Veneto* ▶

80 g ox marrow, 300 g breadcrumbs, about 3 dl meat stock, salt, freshly ground pepper.

This typical sauce from the Veneto region requires the use of a deep earthenware pot. Breadcrumbs are obtained from grating the small rolls called "rosette" or similar bread not containing milk and a stock is made from mixed meats and then strained and skimmed.

◆ Place the pot on the heat protected by a heat-diffuser plate. Melt the ox marrow, sprinkle in the breadcrumbs and stir so that they absorb the fat well.

◆ Add the meat stock, stirring carefully so that no lumps form; leave to simmer over a low heat for 2-3 hours, stirring now and then. Season to taste with salt and freshly ground pepper and remove from the heat.

39

◆ If you wish you may reduce the amount of marrow and flavour the breadcrumbs in melted butter or oil. You may also substitute the pepper with freshly grated radish and add some grated Parmesan before removing from heat. Traditionally the sauce is used to accompany mixed boiled meats. Each guest pours a generous helping of the sauce onto the sliced meat.

FIRST COURSES

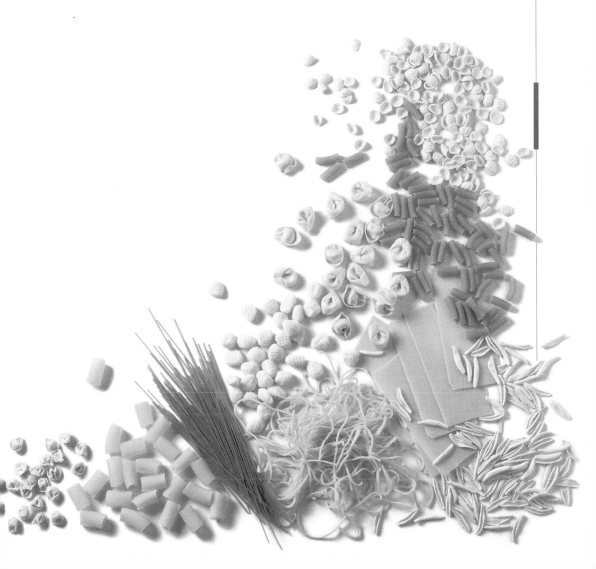

ACQUA COTTA

◀ Tuscany ▶ 📷

2 onions, 2 tomatoes, 1 stalk of celery, 1 egg per guest, rosemary, extra virgin olive oil, salt, slices of toasted bread.
This soup is also made in other regions and ingredients vary according to the vegetables in season.

In a slightly oiled earthenware pot, stew the sliced onions, the celery and fresh tomatoes. After about 30 minutes add some hot water to the vegetables with salt and some chopped rosemary. While the soup comes to the boil (5 minutes should be enough) place a slice of toasted bread in each soup plate. Beat the eggs and pour them over the slices of toast. Pour the hot soup over the bread and beaten egg.

TRUFFLE AGNOLOTTI
(RAVIOLI)

◀ Valle d'Aosta-Piedmont ▶

For the pastry: 400 g of flour, 4 eggs, salt.
For the filling: 150 g lean pork, 150 g Parma ham, 100 g veal, 50 g butter, half a truffle, 1 egg, dry white wine, a handful of grated Parmesan cheese, salt, pepper.
For flavouring: half a truffle, grated Parmesan, butter.

Cook over a low heat, the butter, minced veal and pork, chopped ham, half the truffle (grated or cut into thin slices), 1 egg, Parmesan cheese, salt and pepper. Mix the ingredients and add a little white wine if necessary. When the mixture is cooked prepare the pasta: knead the ingredients and work to obtain a dough with a firm consistency and a glossy surface. Sprinkle flour over a work table, and using a rolling pin or a pasta making machine, roll out the pasta very thinly. Place little piles of the filling over one half of the pasta, fold over and cut out desired shapes with a pastry cutter. Leave the ravioli to dry on a cloth.
Meanwhile heat salt water in a pot and just when it begins to boil drop in the agnolotti. As soon as they float to the surface remove with a slotted spoon. Place them on a hot serving dish and sprinkle with grated Parmesan. Drizzle with melted butter and dust with the remaining half truffle.

NEAPOLITAN AGNOLOTTI

◀ Campania ▶

For the pastry: 400 g flour, 4 eggs, salt.
For the filling: 300 g ricotta, 2 eggs, 1 large mozzarella, 1 handful of basil leaves, salt, freshly ground pepper.
For the meat sauce: 300 g minced beef, 500 g tomato purée, 1 onion, a few leaves of basil, red wine, extra-virgin olive oil, salt and pepper.

Mix the pasta ingredients together and knead to a firm dough with a glossy surface. Meanwhile prepare the filling by mixing in a bowl the ricotta, eggs, basil, mozzarella, salt and some freshly ground pepper. Cook the meat sauce: soften the onion in oil over a low heat

in an earthenware pot, then add the meat and allow to brown while stirring continuously. Season and add a little wine. After a few minutes add the tomato purée. Cook over a low heat for about an hour and towards the end of the cooking time add the chopped basil and pepper. Roll out the pasta on a floured work table and cut into large circles. In the middle of each place some of the filling then fold the pastry to form agnolotti, pressing the edges down well. Cook the agnolotti in plentiful salt water, strain and serve with the meat sauce and add grated Parmesan or pecorino.

AGNOLOTTI OF FRIULI

◀ Friuli Venezia Giulia ▶

400 g flour, 4 eggs, 400 g potatoes, 1 onion, 3 leaves of mint, cinnamon, 1 small glass of cognac, smoked ricotta, butter, salt, pepper.

Prepare the pasta by mixing together the flour with the eggs and a pinch of salt: knead the dough with your hands, cover with a cloth and leave to rest for about half an hour. Meanwhile prepare the filling, boil and peel the potatoes and mash them, preferably in a food mill. Mix the potato purée with salt, paper, cognac, chopped mint and a pinch of cinnamon. In a pan cook the sliced onion in a little butter: add the potatoes and mix well. Roll out the pastry and cut into squares. Place a little heap of filling on each square, then fold over to

shape the agnolotti. Cook in plenty of salt water and serve flavoured with melted butter and grated smoked ricotta.

FISH SOUP

◀ Marche ▶

1.2 kg mixed fish (dogfish, cod, angler fish, mantis prawn, mullet etc.) 500 g cuttlefish, 1 onion, chopped parsley, 1 pinch saffron or turmeric, 1 full glass dry white wine, 1 dessertspoon vinegar, 1 glass extra-virgin oil, salt, pepper, bread croutons.

Clean the fish and divide the larger ones into regular-size pieces; remove the ink sac, eyes and bone from the cuttlefish and cut into strips. Wash all the fish in plenty of salt water and drain.

Cook the onion in a pot with a little oil; when the onion is transparent add the cuttlefish and the saffron dissolved in a little hot water. As soon as the cuttlefish has become yellow in colour, add salt and pepper and add enough water to cover; leave to cook slowly for half an hour.

Take a wide two-handled saucepan (so you can shift the fish without using ladles or forks).

At the bottom place a layer of mantis prawns, then the cooked cuttlefish and the more solid pieces of fish with the more tender fish pieces at the top. Pour in the cuttlefish cooking liquid while still hot.

Ensure that the fish is completely covered by adding equal measures of wine, vinegar and hot water; season to taste and cook on a rapid heat for a quarter of an hour, shaking the saucepan contents every now and then. Serve the soup quite hot together with the toasted bread croutons.

BUCATINI ALL'AMATRICIANA

◀ *Lazio* ▶

400 g bucatini (type of spaghetti), 200 g lean streaky bacon, 300 g small ripe, firm tomatoes, 1/2 onion, grated pecorino, extra-virgin olive oil, salt, chilli powder.

Cut the bacon into pieces and cook in a few spoonfuls of oil; as soon as the fat has melted, remove from the pan. Cook the finely chopped onion in the bacon fat, then add the tomatoes, skinned, with seeds removed and chopped. Add salt and leave the sauce to thicken for about ten minutes. Add the bacon again and flavour with the red chilli.
Cook the bucatini in boiling salt water and when cooked but still firm, add to the sauce. Sprinkle with grated pecorino.
Tomatoes were not in the original recipe and can be left out.

BUCATINI AMMUDICATI

◀ *Basilicata* ▶

400 g bucatini (type of spaghetti), 5 salted an-

chovies, 100 g breadcrumbs, 1/2 glass of extra-virgin olive oil, salt, pepper.

Remove the salt and bones from the anchovies. Heat the oil in a small pan and melt the anchovies. In another pot, lightly brown the breadcrumbs, stirring with a wooden spoon and season with salt and some good ground pepper. Cook the bucatini in plenty of salt water, drain when al dente and mix the anchovy oil. Sprinkle with breadcrumbs instead of grated cheese and serve.

BUCATINI WITH LAMB SAUCE

◀ *Abruzzo-Molise* ▶

400 g bucatini, 200 g minced lamb, 2 cloves garlic, 1 sprig of rosemary, 2 bay leaves, 400 g tomato purée, red wine, grated pecorino, extra-virgin olive oil, salt, pepper.

Brown the meat in oil together with the garlic (which should be removed when the meat starts to brown), rosemary and bay leaves. Add a little wine and allow to evaporate. Add the tomato purée, salt and pepper to taste and cook over a low heat.
In the meantime cook the bucatini in plentiful salt water, drain and add to the sauce. Sprinkle with grated cheese.

CANEDERLI

◀ *Trentino-Alto Adige* ▶

400 g stale bread, 100 g smoked bacon, 50 g

salami, about 1.5 litres of stock, 2 egg whites flour as required, milk, parsley, extra-virgin olive oil, grated Parmesan cheese, salt.

Cut the bread into small cubes and slightly moisten with milk. Meanwhile cut the bacon and the salami into little cubes and mix with the bread and a little flour, a handful of chopped parsley and the eggs. Season the mixture and work to obtain a consistent batter. Shape some balls the size of a mandarin. Bring the stock to the boil, lower the flame so that it simmers slightly and cook the canederli for about 20 minutes until they float to the top. Serve the canederli in hot meat stock or drain and serve with tomato sauce or butter and grated Parmesan.

CAPPELLETTI IN BROTH

◀ Emilia Romagna ▶

For the stock: 500 g boned beef, 500 g boned veal, 1/2 chicken, 1 onion, peeled and stuck with two cloves, 1 carrot, 1 stalk of celery, 1 tomato, 1 bay leaf, salt, peppercorns.
For the pasta: 400 g flour, 4 eggs, salt.
For the filling: 100 g chicken breast, 100 g pork loin, 100 g veal, 150 g Parma ham, 1 slice of mortadella, 100 g grated Parmesan cheese, 2 eggs, nutmeg, butter, salt, pepper.

First prepare a good stock. Clean the chicken and cook with the other meat in 1.5 litres of water and a pinch of salt over a low heat. As the liquid comes to the boil add the vegetables, some peppercorns and the bay leaf. Leave to simmer slowly for about an

hour and a half, skimming regularly. Remove the meat and filter the broth. Allow to cool, then scrape away the fat on the surface with a spatula.
Cook the chicken breast, pork loin and veal in a little butter. Chop together with the Parma ham and the mortadella, and bind with the eggs, grated cheese, a pinch of nutmeg and, finally, the salt and pepper.
Prepare the pasta by kneading the ingredients together to obtain a glossy, smooth dough. On a floured work surface and with a rolling pin or pasta making machine roll out to thin sheets. Cut into little squares, drop a little filling onto each, and fold the squares over to form triangles. Wrap the outer ends around a finger and turn over the third corner. Cook the cappelletti in the meat broth and sprinkle with grated Parmesan.

CASONCELLI

◀ Lombardy ▶

For the pasta: 500 g of white flour, 1 pinch of salt, 4 eggs, 1 yolk.
For the filling: 300 g beef, 1 carrot, 1 small stalk of celery, 1/2 onion, 1 clove, 1 pinch of nutmeg, 3-4 basil leaves, 1 egg yolk, 1/2 glass full bodied red wine, 50 g grated Parmesan cheese, 50 g fine breadcrumbs, butter, 2 dessertspoons of extra-virgin olive oil, salt, pepper.
For flavouring: a few sage leaves, 100 g grated Parmesan, 120 g butter.

First prepare the dough by kneading the flour with a pinch of salt, the eggs and, if necessary, a little water. Knead

soup tureen, flavoured with the melted butter, sage and grated cheese. Allow to rest for a few seconds before serving to allow the flavours to blend.

CAVATIEDDI WITH ROCKET

◀ Puglia ▶

For the cavatieddi (type of pasta): 250 g white flour, 100 g durum wheat flour, salt.
For the sauce: 500 g ripe, firm tomatoes, 300 g rocket, 1 clove garlic, extra-virgin olive oil, matured ricotta, salt, chilli powder.

Mix the flour together with a pinch of salt and knead with a little lukewarm water to obtain a soft uniform dough. Divide into cylinders of about 1/2 centimetre in diameter. Cut the cylinders into small tubes. With the rounded blade of a knife, form each tube into a small elongated shell. Allow to dry on a cloth which has been sprinkled with flour.

Skin the tomatoes, remove the seeds and chop into large pieces. In a pan heat the oil and add the crushed garlic, add the tomatoes, flavour with salt and chilli powder. Allow the sauce to thicken over a moderate heat for about 15 minutes.

Clean the rocket, cook for a few seconds in boiling salt water, remove and

47

well for about 10 minutes and roll out 2 thin sheets. Be careful not to let them dry.

In a pan, cook the finely sliced onion with a large knob of butter and the extra-virgin olive oil, add the meat and brown on all sides, then add the wine and allow to evaporate. Cut the vegetables into small pieces and add to the pot with the garlic clove, the chopped basil, salt, pepper and a pinch of nutmeg, and cook covered for about two hours, adding a little hot water from time to time if required.

When cooked, chop the meat and sieve the vegetables. In a bowl mix the filling with the breadcrumbs, the grated cheese and the egg yolk and season to taste.

On a sheet of pastry make small piles of the prepared filling about one finger's width apart and cover with another sheet. With your fingers press down around each small heap so as to seal it off well. With a pastry cutter divide into pieces about 4cm square and leave to dry on a cloth sprinkled lightly with flour. When ready to serve cook the casoncelli for about 10 minutes in salt water, strain and serve in a warmed

rinse, squeeze and chop finely. In the same water used for cooking the rocket cook the cavatieddi and strain when cooked but still firm. Spoon into the tomato sauce and add the rocket. Mix and serve with sprinkled grated ricotta and chilli powder.

CIUPPIN

◄ Liguria ►

1.5 kg mixed fish (scorpion fish, John Dory, anchovies...) 4 ripe, firm tomatoes, 1 medium sized onion, 1 carrot, 1/2 stalk of celery, 1 sprig of parsley, 1 clove of garlic, 1 glass of dry white wine, extra-virgin olive oil, salt, pepper, slices of bread.

Skin the tomatoes, remove the seeds and chop and put aside. Peel and finely chop the onion, carrot, celery and garlic, then cook these in a pot with a few dessertspoons of oil. When the onion has become transparent add the wine and allow to evaporate. Add the chopped tomatoes and stir for a few seconds. Add 1.5 litres of boiling salt water and cook over a moderate heat for about 15 minutes.
Meanwhile clean and rinse the fish and cut into pieces. Add to the broth beginning with the firmer, fleshier varieties as they take longer to cook, and adding the others later. Season and continue to cook for another 15 minutes.
Remove the soup from the heat and pressing down well with a wooden spoon so as to obtain a purée (ciuppin). Replace over the heat in an earthenware pot. Season and sprinkle with finely chopped parsley. If the soup is too thick dilute with a few ladles of hot salt water. As the soup comes to the boil again, remove from heat, serve with some slices of bread toasted in the oven or heated in a pan slightly greased with oil.

POTATO CULINGIONIS

◄ Sardinia ►

For the pastry: 500 g flour, lard, salt.
For the filling: 600 g potatoes, 300 g grated strong-flavoured pecorino, 2 cloves of garlic, mint, salt.
For flavouring: 300 g tomato sauce, 100 g matured pecorino.

Form a well with the flour, add lard and water to obtain a soft dough. Knead well and allow to rest for a time under a tea-cloth. Meanwhile boil the potatoes, peel and mash them in a soup tureen. Add the grated pecorino, a few chopped mint leaves and garlic and salt to taste. Roll out the dough to obtain a thin sheet of pastry and cut out some circles of about 7 centimetres in diameter. Drop a small quantity of the potato mixture in the centre of the circles, fold them over and close them, pinching the edges. Cook the culingionis in salt water, drain and add tomato sauce and sprinkle with grated pecorino. Place in a hot oven for ten minutes before serving.

FUSILLI WITH BROAD BEANS

◀ Basilicata ▶

400 g fusilli (curly pasta), 400 g fresh broad beans, 400 g ripe, firm tomatoes, 2 cloves of garlic, a few leaves of basil, extra-virgin olive oil, salt, chilli powder.

Clean the broad beans by eliminating the small black "eye". Plunge the tomatoes into hot water, peel them, remove their seeds and chop roughly. Heat a few spoonfuls of oil in a pan, add a clove of garlic and then the beans. After a few minutes add the tomatoes. Flavour with salt and a pinch of chilli powder and continue to cook over a moderate heat, adding a little hot water from time to time. Before removing from heat add a few leaves of basil. Boil the pasta in salt water and strain when it is al dente. Flavour with the broad bean sauce and a little oil.

GNOCCHI ALLA VALDOSTANA

◀ Valle d'Aosta-Piedmont ▶

200 g maize meal, 100 g cornflour, 150 g fontina (cheese from Val d'Aosta), 2 eggs, 1 litre of milk, nutmeg, grated Parmesan, butter, salt, pepper.

Heat the milk in a pot and when it comes to the boil add both types of flour, stirring constantly. When it is cooked (after about 40 minutes) add the cheese cut into small cubes, a spoonful of butter and a pinch of nutmeg. Mix well.
Allow the mixture to cool, then fold in the two egg yolks. Roll the mixture out to a thickness of one centimetre. Cut out some circles using a glass of 4cm to 5 cm in diameter and lay them in an overlapping pattern on the base of a greased rectangular Pyrex dish.
Dust with grated Parmesan and pepper,

49

add some melted butter and bake in a moderate oven for ten minutes.

POTATO GNOCCHI

◀ *Veneto* ▶

For the gnocchi: 1 kg. potatoes, about 200 g flour, a few sage leaves, butter, salt.
For the sauce: 800 g ripe, firm tomatoes, 1 small bunch of basil, 1/2 teaspoon sugar, extra-virgin olive oil, salt, pepper.

Boil the potatoes, then peel and mash them while still hot. On a pastry board, knead the potatoes gently with the salt and flour to obtain a soft, pliable dough. Form cylinders about the size of a finger and then cut into small pieces to make small dumplings. Pass these over a grater to obtain the rough exterior typical of gnocchi.

Prepare a tomato sauce: wash the tomatoes, plunge them into boiling water, skin them and remove any stems and seeds. Blend in a food processor. If there is a lot of liquid, let the tomatoes drain on a sloping surface for about 15 minutes before blending. Cook the purée over a moderate heat with a little oil and leave to thicken for about 30 minutes with a pinch of salt and one of sugar and stirring from time to time. Just before removing from the heat season with pepper and finely chopped basil.

In a separate pot melt a generous amount of butter and add a couple of sage leaves.

Bring some salt water to boil in a large pot then drop in the dumplings a few at a time. As soon as they rise to the surface remove them with a slotted spoon and arrange them on plates. Add the tomato sauce and a little melted butter and sage.

The gnocchi can also be flavoured with meat sauce, gorgonzola or simply with melted butter and cinnamon.

JOTA

◀ *Friuli Venezia Giulia* ▶

500 g sauerkraut, 200 g dried borlotti beans, 2 potatoes, 2 dessertspoons flour, 300 g bacon, 2 bay leaves, 1 pinch cumin seeds, 1/2 glass of extra-virgin olive oil, salt, pepper.

Steep the beans in water for 12 hours, then rinse, change the water and boil them. After about an hour add the potatoes which have been peeled and cut into large slices. In another pot toast some flour in oil, taking care not to burn it. When it is golden brown

add the sauerkraut, the bacon cut into small cubes, the cumin seeds, bay leaves, salt and pepper.

Add enough water just to cover the mixture and cook until the liquid has dried. Add this mixture to the beans and potatoes and continue to cook for other 20 minutes. Stir now and then and salt to taste.

Before serving let the jota rest for a while: it can even be prepared the day before.

BAKED LASAGNE

◀ *Emilia Romagna* ▶ 📷

For the pasta: 400 g flour, 4 eggs, salt.
For the béchamel: 50 g butter, 50 g flour, 1/2 litre milk, nutmeg, salt, pepper.
For the sauce: 150 g minced meat, 1 slice cooked ham, about 50 g in weight, 50 g sausage, 300 g tomato pulp, 1/2 onion, 1/2 carrot, 1/2 stalk celery, 1 clove of garlic, bay leaves, sage, basil, 1 clove, cinnamon, 1/2 glass of red wine, extra-virgin olive oil, salt, pepper.
For blending: 2 mozzarella cheeses, grated Parmesan, butter, salt.

Prepare the pasta by kneading the ingredients into a glossy, smooth dough. Sprinkle flour onto a work surface and roll out the dough to a very thin sheet of pastry. Cut into rectangles about 8cm x 16cm in size. Bring a pot of salt water to the boil and cook the pasta sheets for a few minutes. Strain the pasta and dip into a dish of cold water to halt the cooking process and lay out on some kitchen towels to dry.
Prepare the sauce: peel the onion and

garlic and chop with the carrot, celery and ham. In a pan brown the sausage in a little oil and add the chopped vegetables and ham. Allow the mixture to soften, stirring constantly. Add the minced meat and let it brown evenly. Add a little wine, allow to evaporate, then the tomatoes, bay leaves and salt. Lower the heat and allow to simmer for about one hour, keeping it covered.

Meanwhile prepare the béchamel: in a pot melt the butter over a low heat and blend the flour in well with the help of a wooden spoon. At the same time have the milk heating in a separate pan but do not allow it to boil. Add the hot milk a little at a time to the butter and flour to avoid lumps forming. At this point you can substitute the wooden spoon with an egg beater. Continue stirring until the liquid begins to thicken. The sauce is ready 10 minutes after the first bubbles start to form. Before removing from the heat add the salt, pepper and a little nutmeg. To make a thicker sauce you can increase the amounts of butter and flour, ensuring however, that the measures are always equal, without changing the quantity of milk.

On the bottom of a greased rectangular oven pan spread some sauce and a little béchamel, mixing them with a wooden spoon.

Add first a layer of lasagne and sprinkle with diced mozzarella and Parmesan cheese; make another layer of pasta and spread it with the sauce and the béchamel. Continue in this way, alter-

nating the ingredients until they are finished, ending with the sauce and béchamel. Dust with Parmesan cheese, add a few flakes of butter and bake in a hot oven for about 40 minutes.

MACARONI WITH *RICOTTA* AND SAUSAGE

◄ *Calabria* ►

400 g macaroni, 400 g of fresh ricotta, 200 g sausage, grated pecorino, salt, freshly ground pepper.

Skin the sausage, cook it over a low het in a pan with a little water so that it does not brown. In a soup tureen mash the ricotta with a fork then add the sausage, salt and plenty of freshly ground pepper. Cook the pasta in salt water; when it is al dente, strain it but leave a little cooking water. Mix in the ricotta and sprinkle with grated pecorino.

MALLOREDDUS

◄ *Sardinia* ►

250 g durum wheat flour, 150 g white flour, saffron, salt.

Dissolve the saffron in a cup and a half of lukewarm water. On a pastry board mix the flour and form a well. Into the centre pour the water and saffron. Add a pinch of salt and mix it all carefully. When the dough is smooth, shape into small rolls and then divide these into lengths of about two centimetres. Roll the malloreddus along the back of a

grater to give them their traditional pattern.

Lay them on trays to dry. These can only be used once they are very dry and it is advisable to prepare them a few days beforehand. The maloreddus can be served with a variety of sauces.

MILLE COSEDDE

◄ *Calabria* ►

350 g short pasta, 150 g dried broad beans, 150 g dried chickpeas, 150 g dried beans, 1/2 savoy cabbage, 1 onion, 1 carrot, 1 celery stalk, 50 g smoked bacon, grated pecorino, extra-virgin olive oil, salt, pepper, chilli powder.

Steep the legumes in water overnight. Change the water and boil them, adding salt only at the end of the cooking time.

Clean the savoy of its outer leaves and cut it finely. Chop the carrot, the onion, celery and bacon and cook together in plenty of oil. Continue cooking over a moderate heat and add the strained legumes, the savoy and 2 litres of water. Salt to taste and add the chilli powder. As soon as it comes to the boil add the pasta. When the pasta is al dente remove from heat and sprinkle lavishly with grated pecorino cheese.

MINESTRA MARITATA (VEGETABLE AND CHEESE HOT-POT)

◄ *Campania* ►

500 g endive, 500 g chicory, 1/2 head cabbage, 2 celery stalks, 350 g fennel, 100 g lard, 100 g sea-

soned caciocavallo (gourd shaped cheese from southern Italy), 3/4 litre stock, salt, chilli powder.

Blanch the endive, chicory, cabbage, celery and fennel separately in hot water for a few minutes only so that they remain firm. Strain and chop roughly. Bring the stock to boil with the lard cut into small cubes and allow to simmer for about ten minutes. Form a layer of vegetables in an earthenware pot. Follow with a layer of caciocavallo cut into cubes. Add the stock. Cover and allow to cook for 15-20 minutes over a moderate flame. Before serving allow the soup to rest for 15 minutes with the lid still on. Pork sausage can be added to vary this recipe.

SARDINIAN *MINESTRONE*

◀ *Sardinia* ▶

1.5 kg vegetables in season, 200 g malloreddus (see recipe), wild fennel, extra-virgin olive oil, salt, freshly ground pepper.

Peel and wash the vegetables and chop into small pieces. Place them in a pot and cover with cold water. Add a sprig of wild fennel, salt and some ground pepper. Place over a low heat and cook for about an hour and a half. 30 minutes before the end of cooking time, add the malloreddus. Serve with a drizzle of oil.

ORECCHIETTE WITH BROCCOLI

◀ *Puglia* ▶

For the orecchiette: 350 g white flour, 100 g durum wheat flour, salt.

For the sauce: 300 g broccoli, 2 cloves garlic, 1 dessertspoon raisins (optional), 1 spoonful pine nuts (optional), 2 salted anchovies, grated pecorino, extra-virgin olive oil, salt, chilli powder.

Start by preparing the dough for the orecchiette. On a floured work surface, mix the two kinds of flour, add a pinch of salt and form a well. Add lukewarm water and knead to obtain a firm, uniform dough. After kneading for about 10 minutes, shape the dough into long rolls a few centimetres in diameter. Cut off several small pieces about 1 centimetre long and with the blade of a knife bend the pieces into little shells. With your thumb dent the shells to give them the shape of orecchiette or 'little ears'. Allow to rest on a cloth lightly sprinkled with flour.

Carefully wash the broccoli and cook in salt water until they are al dente. Remove the vegetables but keep the water aside. Cook the crushed garlic in a few spoonfuls of oil, and blend in the cleaned anchovies. Add the broccoli and bring to the boil, adding some hot salt water if necessary. Before removing from the heat check the seasoning, add chilli powder, pine seeds and raisins which have been steeped in lukewarm water and dried.

Cook the orecchiette in the same water used to cook the vegetables until they are al dente and stir them in the vegetable mixture. Sprinkle with grated or diced pecorino cheese.

PANCOTTO
(COOKED BREAD)
◄ *Liguria* ►

400 g stale bread, butter, grated Parmesan, 2 egg yolks., 1.5 litres of meat stock made from: 500 g beef, 500 g veal, 1/2 chicken, 1 onion, peeled and stuck with 1 or 2 cloves, 1 carrot, 1 stalk of celery, 1 tomato, 1 bay leaf, salt, a few peppercorns.

To prepare the stock, clean the chicken and place it with the other meat in a large pot with 1.5 litres of cold water and a pinch of salt. Cook over a moderate heat and as it comes to the boil add the onion, celery and tomato, a few peppercorns and the bay leaf.

Allow to simmer slowly for about an hour and a half, skimming at regular intervals. Once it is cooked remove the meat and sieve the stock. To remove the fat completely allow the stock to cool and skim off the layer of solid fat with a wooden spatula

In a pot boil the stock for about ten minutes with the stale bread cut into small cubes and a knob of butter. Remove from the heat, mix in the egg yolks and flavour with a generous helping of grated Parmesan.

PANSOTTI WITH NUTS

◀ *Liguria* ▶

For the pastry: 500 g flour, 3 eggs.
For the filling: 300 g ricotta, 500 g chard, 500 g preboggion (1 head of cabbage, chard leaves and parsley), 1 bunch of borage, 3 eggs, 50 g Parmesan, nutmeg, salt.
For flavouring: walnuts, pine-nuts, 1 clove of garlic, extra-virgin olive oil.

Wash the vegetables, cook them in boiling salt water, drain and chop. In a bowl mix together the ricotta, the grated Parmesan, eggs, salt and some grated nutmeg. Lastly add the chopped cooked vegetables.
Prepare the sauce by chopping the walnuts, pine-nuts and garlic and crushing them together in the mortar. (Use a little oil to obtain a smooth sauce).
Prepare the pasta and divide it into portions about 6cm square.
Drop a little heap of filling into the centre of each square, fold over the pasta into a triangle and press the edges together.
Cook the pansotti in boiling salt water, strain and arrange on a warm serving dish. Cover immediately with the walnut sauce.

PAPPARDELLE WITH HARE SAUCE

◀ *Tuscany* ▶

400 g fresh pappardelle, 1 saddle of hare, boned, 1 slice of Parma ham, about 50 g in weight, 100 g tomato purée, 1 onion, 1 carrot, 1 celery stalk, 1 bay leaf, 1 spoonful of parsley, thyme and rosemary chopped together, 4 juniper berries, 1 glass of red wine, stock, extra-virgin olive oil, salt, pepper.

Fry all the finely chopped herbs and vegetables and when the onion starts to brown add some chopped ham and the hare meat cut into pieces. Stir for a while, allowing the flavours to blend, then add a little red wine and allow to evaporate.
When the meat starts to dry out, pour in the tomato purée and continue cooking for about an hour and a half, keeping the sauce moist with a little hot stock (or a glass of milk).
Cook the pappardelle in plentiful salt water, strain when al dente and serve in a warm soup tureen. Add the sauce and garnish with pieces of meat.

PASTA ALLA NORMA

◀ *Sicily* ▶

400 g pasta, 100 g salted ricotta, 4 aubergines, 500 g tomato pulp, 1 onion, 40 g fresh pork fat, extra-virgin olive oil, salt, pepper.

Prepare the sauce by cooking the sliced onion in a pan with the pork fat and a few spoonfuls of oil. Add the tomato pulp, salt and pepper and cook over a moderate heat for 20 minutes.

Meanwhile slice the aubergines, dust with salt and leave them to drain for half an hour in a colander so that they lose their bitterness. Rinse and dry them, then cook them in oil on both sides. Drain with a slotted spoon and leave to dry, sprinkled with salt, on kitchen paper.

Cook the pasta in plentiful salt water and strain when al dente, add the tomato sauce and sprinkle with ricotta. Garnish each portion with fried aubergine and serve immediately.

PASTA WITH CHICKPEAS

◀ *Lazio* ▶

300 g short pasta, 200 g chickpeas, 5 cloves of garlic, 4 ripe tomatoes, 1 sprig of rosemary, a few anchovy fillets, extra-virgin olive oil, salt, freshly ground pepper.

Steep the chickpeas for about 24 hours. Rinse and place in a pot together with three whole cloves of garlic, a sprig of rosemary and enough clean water to cover.

Add salt and pepper and leave to cook over a moderate flame for about three hours. Meanwhile, in a small pan, cook the remaining garlic together with the skinned and chopped tomatoes and a few little pieces of anchovy fillets.

When the chickpeas are cooked, add the sauce to the pot; add some hot water if necessary and when it comes to the boil again add the pasta.

Before serving, remove the sprig of rosemary and the cloves of garlic, sprinkle with some ground pepper and drizzle with oil.

PASTA AND BEANS

◀ *Veneto* ▶ 📷

200 g tagliatelle (type of pasta), 300 g of dry borlotti beans, 1 carrot, 1 onion, 1 stalk of celery, 1 clove of garlic, 1 sprig of rosemary or sage, 100 g pork rind, grated cheese 1/2 glass of extra-virgin olive oil, salt, pepper.

Steep the beans in water for 12 hours. Blanch the pork rind for 5 minutes in boiling water, drain and scrape well. Peel and chop the onion and the other vegetables and cook them together with the garlic and rosemary and/or sage in a little oil. Rinse the beans and add to the vegetable mixture. Add the pork rind and about 1.5 litres of water. Add salt and cook, covered, over a low heat, for about 2-3 hours. Remove some of the beans (half, or a third if you prefer a thicker soup), pass through a food mill, and replace in the soup.

Cook the tagliatelle in the soup mixture which should be diluted with a few ladles of boiling water if necessary. Before serving, remove the pork rind and slice it into thin strips, placing one in each bowl. Ladle out the bean soup, flavour with freshly ground pepper, add a trickle of fresh oil and a sprinkle of grated cheese.

This is just one of the many versions of pasta and beans.

The soup can also be flavoured with tomato purée or concentrate and the tagliatelle substituted with mixed pasta leftovers. The pork rind need not be used.

PENNE ALL'ARRABBIATA

◀ Calabria ▶

400 g penne (type of macaroni), 500 g ripe, firm tomatoes, 2 cloves of garlic, 1 whole red chilli pepper, grated pecorino, extra-virgin olive oil, salt.

Cook the cloves of garlic in two dessertspoons of oil. Add the skinned and diced tomatoes. Let the sauce thicken slowly, then season with salt and the crumbled red chilli. Continue to cook over a moderate heat for about 20 minutes, stirring now and then. Meanwhile cook the pasta in salt water and strain when al dente. Add the pasta to the spicy sauce while it is still cooking. Before serving, flavour with plenty of grated pecorino.

PICI WITH RABBIT

◀ Tuscany ▶

For the pici: 500 g flour, 1 egg, 1 dessertspoon of extra-virgin olive oil, salt.
For the sauce: 1/2 a rabbit, 300 g tomato sauce, 100 g bacon, 1 onion, 1 carrot, 2 stalks of celery, 2 cloves of garlic, 2 bay leaves, 1/2 litre of red wine, extra-virgin olive oil, salt, pepper.

Steep the rabbit in a marinade of aromatic herbs and vegetables for a few hours. When ready to cook, strain the vegetables and chop them finely. Cook them in a little oil with some chopped bacon. Remove the rabbit from the marinade and cut it into pieces. Add it to the vegetables as they start to turn golden brown. Allow the meat to cook for a little, add the wine and allow to evaporate almost completely. Add the tomato sauce. Check the seasoning, cover the pot and continue to cook over a moderate heat for half an hour.
When the sauce is ready, take the rabbit out, drain it and remove the bones. Cut the meat into small pieces. Stir the cooking liquid to make it creamy, and replace the small pieces of meat. Cover and leave to rest while preparing the pasta.
Pici is a kind of home-made pasta typical of Siena. The dough is rolled out on the pastry board and able pasta-makers are then able to stretch it by hand to a couple of metres in length.
Start by making a well of the flour on the pastry board, break the egg in the centre, add the oil and a little lukewarm water. Knead the dough vigorously, gradually adding a little lukewarm water if necessary. When the dough is firm and smooth, make a small loaf, brush oil over the surface and leave to rest under a cloth for half an hour. Roll out a sheet of pastry and cut into small strips. Roll these with your hands, giving each one the shape of a small piece of string. Allow the pici to dry on a floured cloth or lightly sprinkle with flour so that the pieces don't stick together.

Boil the pici in salt water, drain when the pasta is al dente and mix into the rabbit sauce as it is being warmed over a low heat.

BAKED *PIZZOCCHERI*

◀ *Lombardy* ▶

300 g pizzoccheri, 150 g grated Parmesan cheese, 150 g soft cheese like fontina (from Val d'Aosta), or "bitto", 200 g savoy cabbage or chard, 200 g potatoes, 3 cloves of garlic, 1 sprig of sage, 100 g butter, extra-virgin olive oil, salt.

Wash and cut the savoy and potatoes into pieces and boil both in plenty of salt water. In the same pot cook the pizzoccheri. Timing should be accurate so that the pasta and vegetables can be drained together when they are al dente. Meanwhile cut the soft cheese into thin strips. Melt the butter with a few dessertspoons of oil, flavour with the sage and the crushed cloves of garlic (remove this as it starts to turn brown).

In a Pyrex dish place the first layer of pasta mixed with vegetables, sprinkle a mixture of Parmesan and fontina cheese on the surface and flavour with the sage butter. Continue with another layer of pasta and the other ingredients one by one. Top off with a generous sprinkling of Parmesan and a few flakes of butter and leave to cook in a hot oven for about 10 minutes.

Some versions of this recipe skip the oven stage. The pasta and vegetables are drained and mixed together with the cheese and melted butter and served immediately.

QUADRETTI IN BROTH WITH CHICKEN LIVERS

◀ Emilia Romagna ▶ 📷

200 g egg quadretti, 150 g chicken livers, 1 litre of meat stock, 3 eggs, 1 clove of garlic, 4 sage leaves, 60 g butter, rosemary, 50 g grated Parmesan, salt.

Nowadays, egg quadretti can easily be bought in the shops, whereas once they were obtained from dough left over from the preparation of tagliatelle or cappelletti.

Clean the livers well and cook them in a pan with about a third of the butter, the garlic and sage. Once they have browned remove them from the pan and chop them into very small pieces. Remove the garlic and sage from the pan and return the chicken livers. Continue to cook with the remaining butter, rosemary and salt.

In a pot bring the stock to boil, add the livers and cook for 2 minutes. Add the quadretti and cook for a few minutes more. Stir with a wooden spoon and dust with some grated Parmesan.

RIBOLLITA

◀ Tuscany ▶

500 g stale bread, 150 g dried white beans, 250 g ripe tomatoes, 1 carrot, 1 Tuscan black cabbage, 1 potato, 1 onion, 2 cloves of garlic, 1 stalk of celery, a few sprigs of parsley, thyme, extra-virgin olive oil, salt, chilli powder.

There are many versions of this traditional Tuscan dish, depending on the season and the availability of ingredients. Start by preparing a good bean soup. Leave the dried beans to steep for at least 12 hours, then drain them. Cover with fresh water and cook over a low heat in a covered pot. Meanwhile in a pan cook the diced onion, carrot and celery in a little oil. Add the crushed garlic, the skinned and chopped tomatoes, the red chilli and the thyme and after about 5 minutes add the potatoes cut into small cubes and the thinly sliced cabbage. Cook over a low heat, adding a little water. Pass the beans and their liquid through a food mill and add this mixture to the vegetables. Check the seasoning just before removing from the heat, after about 20 minutes. Meanwhile, in a large ovenproof dish arrange two thin layers of bread and pour the soup over them. Make another two layers of bread and cover with more soup. The ribollita, which means 're-boiled', is obtained by reheating the soup over a very low heat. Make a dent in the centre, add some olive oil and boil very slowly, protecting the pot with a heat-diffuser plate.

RISO ALL'ISOLANA

◀ Veneto ▶

400 g rice, about 1.5 litres of stock, 200 g pork, (preferably the upper part of the leg), 80 g butter, 100 g grated Parmesan, rosemary and cinnamon (optional), salt, freshly ground pepper.

Cut the pork into small cubes, season with salt and freshly ground pepper and allow to rest for about an hour.

Melt the butter over a low heat and add the meat. Continue cooking over a low heat. It can be seasoned with a sprig of rosemary which can be removed before serving. Rinse the rice and cook it in the stock (about 20 minutes) until the latter is completely absorbed and the rice is cooked but firm. If the stock dries before the rice is cooked, add more. Add the hot meat to the rice and mix together. Serve sprinkled with grated Parmesan cheese and, if desired, a pinch of cinnamon.

RICE WITH PORK CHOPS

◀ Lombardy ▶

400 g rice, 4 pork chops, butter, oil or lard, 1 white onion, grated Parmesan cheese, salt, pepper.

In a copper pot if possible, bring to the boil 2 litres of water or double the volume of rice. Slowly pour in the rice so as to make a cone, the tip of which emerges from the water. Shake the pot a couple of times to redistribute the rice, cover and cook over a rapid heat for 10 to 12 minutes. Remove from the heat, stir well and cover with a thick tea-cloth and the lid on top. Allow to rest for

about 15 minutes. Meanwhile cook the pork chops in oil and place one on each plate. Cook the diced onion in the butter, add salt and pepper and add to the rice with the grated Parmesan. Ladle the rice onto the pork chops in the individual plates.

RISOTTO WITH MUSHROOMS

◀ Valle d'Aosta-Piedmont ▶

400 g rice, 300 g mushrooms (the recipe is better if different varieties are used), 1 onion, 1 clove of garlic, parsley, about 1 litre of stock or hot water as required, grated Parmesan, butter, extra-virgin olive oil, salt, pepper.

Slice the onion finely, peel the garlic and cook together in a few spoonfuls of oil with a small piece of butter. Remove the garlic, add the mushrooms which have been rinsed under running water and sliced, and some finely chopped parsley. Flavour with a little salt and pepper and cook for about 30 minutes, adding some hot stock (or water) if necessary. Add the rice and cook, adding the stock a ladle at a time as it becomes absorbed. Once the rice is cooked, sprinkle with grated Parmesan and add a knob of butter, stir well and leave to rest for a minute. Transfer the risotto to a soup tureen and sprinkle with chopped parsley before serving.

RISOTTO WITH SAFFRON

◀ Lombardy ▶

400 g rice, 1/2 onion, 1 small packet of saffron,

stock as required, 50 g beef marrow, 50 g butter, grated Parmesan, salt.

In a pot cook the finely sliced onion with half the butter and the bone marrow. As soon as the onion is transparent, add the rice and stir so that it absorbs the flavour. Add salt and cook by adding the hot stock a ladle at a time and stirring continuously. Three or four minutes from the end add the saffron dissolved in a little hot stock. Remove from heat when the rice is cooked but firm and stir in a generous helping of grated Parmesan and the remaining butter. Cover and allow to rest for a few minutes before serving. According to Milanese tradition this risotto can be served on its own or with "ossibuco Milanese", another typical dish of the area.

SAGNE CHINE

◀ Calabria ▶

For the pasta: 400 g white flour, salt.
For the meatballs: 150 g lean minced pork, 2 dessertspoons grated pecorino, 1 egg, salt, pepper.
For the sauce: 500 g ripe, firm, tomatoes, 200 g fresh porcine mushrooms (or 20 g dried mushrooms), 1 medium sized onion, 1 carrot, 1/2 celery stalk, 1 sprig parsley, 1 lemon, extra-virgin olive oil, salt.
For the filling: 2 artichokes, 1 sprig of parsley, 1 clove of garlic, 1 lemon, 2-3 eggs, 100 g of scamorza cheese, grated pecorino, extra-virgin olive oil, salt.

Prepare the pasta for the lasagne by vigorously kneading the white flour and salt with sufficient water to make a smooth, elastic dough. On a floured work surface roll out a sheet of pastry only a few millimetres thick. Cut out rectangles of pasta measuring about 12 x 7 centimetres.

Cook this pasta in boiling salt water with a little oil added so that the pieces don't stick together. After a few minutes drain and lay on a tea-cloth to dry. Now prepare the meatballs: in a bowl mix the meat with the beaten egg, pecorino, salt and pepper. With wet hands shape them into small meatballs and cook in oil until they are golden brown. Remove from the heat and leave to dry on kitchen paper.

Make the sauce by chopping the onion and vegetables and cooking in a little oil with the cleaned, chopped mushrooms. Plunge the tomatoes into hot water to remove the skins, discard the seeds and chop roughly. Add the tomatoes to the vegetables, add salt and pepper, lower the heat and continue cooking. A few minutes before removing from the heat add a little chopped parsley.

Clean the artichokes and cut into thin slices. Place in some water and lemon juice. Meanwhile simmer a garlic clove in a little oil. Strain the artichokes and add to the oil, removing the garlic at the same time. Add salt and pepper and cook until tender. Add a little parsley and remove from heat.

Dice the scamorza cheese, hard boil the eggs, shell them and cut into slices. When these initial preparations have been completed, begin preparing the sagne chine

Spread the base of a heat resistant dish with a little mushroom sauce and cover with a layer of pasta. Spread a layer of sauce, meatballs, artichokes, hard boiled eggs, scamorza and grated pecorino.

Continue alternating layers of pasta, sauce and filling until you have placed the last sheet of pasta. Cover this with sauce and grated pecorino. Cook the lasagna for thirty to forty minutes in a preheated oven (180°).

There are many versions of this recipe. Peas can be used instead of eggs and in place of the artichokes you can use sausage with the skin removed and cooked in a little oil.

RICE SARTÙ

◀ Campania ▶

400 g rice, 300 g minced beef, 200 g chicken livers, 1 sausage, 250 g fresh peas, 25 g dried mushrooms, 60 g grated Parmesan cheese, 1 mozzarella, 3 eggs, 1 onion, 1.5 litres of stock, 2-3 dessertspoons of concentrated tomato purée, white flour, breadcrumbs, 200 g lard, extra-virgin olive oil, salt pepper.

Cook the sliced onion in an ovenproof dish, add the tomato purée diluted in a glass of stock, the

mushrooms which have been softened in water, drained and chopped, the peas, salt, pepper and a piece of sausage. Allow the sauce to cook for about 20 minutes. Meanwhile in a bowl mix the seasoned minced meat together with a beaten egg and grated cheese. Form small balls of the mixture, roll them in flour and cook them in oil. Cook the rice in a large pot with half the sauce, adding a little hot stock when necessary. When the rice has cooked, remove from the heat, mix in 50g lard, 2 eggs and 4 spoonfuls of grated cheese.

Cook the remaining sauce together with the meatballs and 50g lard.

Wash and dry the chicken livers and dip them in a little lard. Cook in a little stock.

Lightly grease a mould with butter, line the base and sides with rice. In the centre make layers of the meat balls, chicken livers, pieces of mozzarella, pieces of sausage, grated cheese. Continue until all the ingredients have been used. Sprinkle the surface of the sartù with some breadcrumbs and a few knobs of lard. Place the mould in the oven at 160° and cook for about half an hour. Remove from heat and overturn the mould onto a serving dish.

SCRIPELLE 'MBUSSE

◀ Abruzzo-Molise ▶

4 eggs, white flour, 1 sprig of parsley, a glass of milk, 1.5 litres of meat stock, 100 g grated pecorino, extra-virgin olive oil, salt, freshly ground pepper.

Mix the eggs, chopped parsley, milk, a pinch of salt and one of pepper. Add a little flour and mix. Heat a pan which has been slightly oiled and cook a small amount of the mixture to golden brown on both sides. Repeat until all the mixture has been used. Dust the little omelettes with grated pecorino and form little rolls. Place two little rolls on each plate, pour over some hot meat stock, sprinkle with some more grated pecorino and serve.

SPAGHETTI WITH WILD ASPARAGUS

◀ Umbria ▶

400 g spaghetti, 200 g wild asparagus tips, 1 clove of garlic, 400 g tomato pulp, extra-virgin oil, salt, freshly ground pepper.

Wild asparagus is recommended for this typical Umbrian recipe. Only the tips of the asparagus are used and these are washed and then cooked with a little oil and garlic over a low heat. After about 10 minutes add the tomato pulp and salt. The sauce is ready when it starts to thicken. Meanwhile bring the water for the pasta to boil. Cook the spaghetti, strain when al dente, and add to the sauce. Add some ground pepper.

SPAGHETTI WITH GARLIC, OIL AND CHILLI

◀ Abruzzo-Molise ▶

400 g spaghetti, 4 cloves of garlic, 1 red chilli pepper, 1 glass of extra-virgin olive oil, salt.

Cook the pasta in plentiful salt water and in the meantime heat the oil with the chopped chilli pepper in a small pan. Add the thinly sliced garlic. Drain the pasta when it is al dente and season with the oil. A milder sauce can be made by removing the chilli before adding the garlic. If a milder garlic taste is desired, leave the garlic to flavour the oil before cooking. Remove the garlic before heating the oil and add the chilli. This dish should be served very hot.

RISOTTO PILÒTA
(with minced salami)

◀ *Veneto* ▶ 📷

400 g rice, 4 small salami or their equivalent in fresh minced salami, about 8 dl stock, grated Parmesan, butter, salt.

◆ Bring the stock to the boil over a rapid heat. Sprinkle in the rice, keeping it covered by the stock. Give the pot a shake and allow to simmer for 12 minutes.

◆ Remove from the heat, cover the pot with two tea-cloths and allow to rest for 15 minutes.

◆ Meanwhile in a small pot, cook the minced salami or the small salami with the skin removed. Add this to the cooked rice, which should be firm and dry with grains which separate easily. Stir carefully and serve.

A "lighter" version of this recipe uses boned pork instead of salami mince. In this case the quantities need to be increased.

SPAGHETTI WITH CUTTLEFISH INK

◀ Veneto ▶

400 g spaghetti, 400 g small cuttlefish and a few ink sacs, 5 ripe tomatoes (optional), 1 clove of garlic, 1 small bunch of parsley, extra-virgin olive oil, salt, chilli powder.

Wash the cuttlefish then chop roughly. Cook some chopped garlic in a little oil, add the cuttlefish and a ladle of hot water and cook for 15 minutes. Add the roughly chopped tomatoes (skinned and with their seeds removed) and when the sauce has thickened, break the ink sacs into the pan. Season with a handful of chopped parsley, salt and red pepper. Allow the sauce to cook for a few minutes before spooning in the cooked spaghetti.

Another version of this recipe does not use tomatoes; the cuttlefish is cooked in white wine or a few ladles of hot stock.

SPAGHETTI AND TOMATO

◀ Campania ▶ 📷

400 g spaghetti, 800 g very ripe tomatoes, grated pecorino (or Parmesan), some basil leaves, a few spoonfuls of extra-virgin olive oil, sugar, salt, chilli powder.

Bring some water to the boil. Drop in the fresh tomatoes, remove immediately and peel off the withered skin. After peeling remove the seeds and pass

through a food mill. If there is a lot of liquid, cut them in half after peeling and allow to drain on a sloping plate for at least 15 minutes before blending. Over a low heat cook the tomato purée with a teaspoonful of sugar to reduce the acidity together with the oil for about 15 minutes. Add some salt and some chilli powder to taste.

Continue cooking until the sauce has thickened (40 minutes should be sufficient). When cooking is complete add the chopped basil.

Bring a pot of salt water to the boil and cook the spaghetti.

When the spaghetti is al dente transfer to a soup tureen, add the tomato sauce and mix well. Serve some grated cheese separately.

SPAGHETTI ALLA CHITARRA WITH MEAT SAUCE

◀ Abruzzo-Molise ▶

(This pasta takes its name from the special guitar-like instrument used to cut the pasta)
For the spaghetti: 400 g flour, 2 dessertspoons of lard, salt.
For the meat sauce: 1 500 g slice of pork, 4 small slices of bacon, lard, 500 g ripe, firm tomatoes, 3 cloves of garlic, 1 sprig of parsley, red wine, fresh pecorino, salt, freshly ground pepper.

Mix the flour with a bit of lard, salt and enough water to obtain a firm but elastic dough. Knead for some time and then divide the dough into portions. Use the special machine to

cut the pasta, pressing the dough against the wires with a rolling pin. If this machine is not available, use a hand-cutter to make long, thin, flat strips of pasta.

Leave the pasta to dry on a tea-cloth sprinkled with flour and prepare the meat sauce. Chop two cloves of garlic with a bit of parsley and mix with the lard and a little freshly ground pepper. Spread the mixture onto the slice of pork which has been beaten flat.

Lay a few pieces of pecorino on the bacon slices. Roll and close with a toothpick or thread. Cook the remaining clove of garlic in a little lard in an earthenware pot and add the meat and bacon rolls to brown. Add a little wine and allow to evaporate. Season with salt and pepper, add the tomatoes, which have been skinned and chopped with seeds removed. Just before the sauce is ready remove the meat and keep it warm.

Cook the spaghetti in salt water, strain when al dente and add the sauce. Serve the meat as a second course.

SPAGHETTI ALLA CARBONARA

◀ Lazio ▶

400 g spaghetti, 200 g streaky bacon, 2 eggs, 2 yolks, 1 clove of garlic, 3 dessertspoons grated Parmesan cheese, 3 dessertspoons grated pecorino, extra-virgin olive oil, salt, freshly ground pepper.

Chop the bacon into small cubes and brown in a pan together with a few spoonfuls of oil and the clove of garlic. Remove the garlic when the bacon begins to brown.

In a warmed soup tureen mix the eggs and yolks together with the grated cheeses, season with salt and freshly ground pepper to obtain a creamy sauce.

The sauce should be prepared while the pasta is cooking. As soon as the pasta is ready, strain and mix with the egg mixture and the crunchy bacon.

CHEESE AND PEPPER SPAGHETTI

◀ Basilicata ▶

400 g spaghetti, 80 g grated, matured pecorino, extra-virgin olive oil (optional), salt, freshly ground pepper.

Cook the spaghetti in salt water. When ready, do not drain completely but leave a little water to melt the pecorino. Transfer to a warmed soup tureen, drizzle with oil, sprinkle with cheese and plenty of freshly ground pepper. Serve immediately. The traditional

recipe does not require the addition of oil: the pasta is flavoured only with the sauce formed from the cheese and cooking liquid.

SPAGHETTI WITH *BOTTARGA*

◄ *Sardinia* ►

400 g spaghetti, 3 slices of bottarga, 1 clove of garlic, 1 sprig of parsley, 1/2 lemon, 3 dessert-spoons of extra-virgin olive oil, pepper.

Bottarga, which looks like a hard salami of a grey-brown colour, is actually mullet eggs preserved in salt. It can be used in fine slices to prepare canapés or grated to flavour simple pasta dishes.

While the spaghetti is cooking, dissolve the bottarga in a little oil in a small pan. Add some of the water from the pasta pot. As soon as it is dissolved add some lemon juice. Strain the pasta and mix with the bottarga sauce. Dust with pepper and some chopped garlic and parsley. If desired, garnish with some more pieces of bottarga.

SPAGHETTI WITH PILCHARDS

◄ *Calabria* ►

400 g spaghetti, 300 g fresh pilchards, 100 g wild fennel, 30 g pine nuts, 20 g raisins, 4 anchovy fillets, 1 onion, extra-virgin olive oil, salt and pepper.

Clean the pilchards and remove the bones. Rinse thoroughly and chop the fennel. Cook the sliced onion in a pan with plenty of oil, adding the fennel, pine-nuts, raisins (which have been

softened in lukewarm water and strained) and the anchovy fillets. After a few minutes add the pilchards and a little warm water. Add salt and pepper and complete the cooking. Cook the spaghetti in salt water, drain when al dente and add the fish sauce.

SPAGHETTI WITH CLAMS

◄ *Lazio* ►

400 g spaghetti, 1 kg clams, 2 cloves of garlic, 1 small bunch of parsley, 1 whole chilli, dry white wine (optional), extra-virgin olive oil, salt.

Clean the clams under running water and leave them in salt water for at least 30 minutes to rinse off any remaining sand. This is important since the sauce is not filtered. Cook and allow to open in a covered pan with plenty of oil, sliced garlic, the whole chilli and, if desired, a little wine. Meanwhile cook the spaghetti in salt water, drain when al dente, and transfer to the pan with the clams. Stir the pasta over a low heat and sprinkle with some chopped garlic and parsley. Remove from the heat and serve.

STRANGOLAPRETI

◄ *Trentino-Alto Adige* ►

300 g spinach, 2 stale bread rolls, 2 eggs, 2 dessertspoons white flour, a few sage leaves, milk as required, grated Parmesan cheese, butter, salt.

Strangolapreti (literally, priest-strangler) is

a typical dish from Alto-Adige which can also be prepared with nettles or chard. Clean the spinach well, then steam or boil in a little salt water. Drain and chop finely. Meanwhile break up the bread and moisten with a little milk. Add the eggs, flour and a pinch of salt. Stir well, then mix in the spinach and form some dumplings the size of a large walnut. Cook these in plentiful salt water until they float up to the surface (it is advisable to cook a few at a time to avoid sticking) and strain them with a slotted spoon. Roll in grated cheese and melted butter seasoned with a few sage leaves and serve.

TAGLIATELLE WITH BLACK TRUFFLE

◀ Umbria ▶

350 g tagliatelle, 200 g black truffle, 80 g anchovy fillets, clove of garlic, 1 sprig parsley, extra-virgin olive oil, salt.

Grate the truffle and chop the parsley, garlic and anchovies. Work the ingredients in a mortar to obtain a smooth paste. Drizzle with oil and allow to rest. Meanwhile cook the tagliatelle in plentiful salt water and drain when al dente. Heat the truffle sauce in a pan and add the pasta. Serve immediately.

TAGLIATELLE WITH BOLOGNESE MEAT SAUCE

◀ Emilia Romagna ▶

For the tagliatelle: 400 g flour, 4 eggs, salt.

For the sauce: 200 g minced beef, 50 g bacon, 1/2 onion, 1 small carrot, 1/2 stalk of celery, 2 dessertspoons of concentrated tomato sauce, 1/2 glass of red wine, stock as required, grated Parmesan cheese, extra-virgin olive oil, salt, pepper.

Bolognese sauce is the most traditional of the Italian meat sauces. For this reason it is suitable for the preparation of first courses as well as polenta etc. To prepare, chop the onion, the carrot and the celery and bacon. Brown the bacon in a few dessertspoons of oil. When the bacon fat has melted, add the chopped vegetables, stirring carefully, and as soon as they have softened, add the minced meat. Keep stirring so that the meat browns evenly. Add a little wine and allow to evaporate. Add the tomato sauce dissolved in a little seasoned hot stock. Lower the heat and cook in a covered pan for around 2 hours, adding a little stock from time to time. The recipe can be varied by the use of mixed meats or by adding chicken livers, flavouring with dry mushrooms and the water in which they have been softened, or by doing without the tomato.

Prepare the pasta and divide into long strips 1cm in width. Leave to dry on a floured surface. Cook the pasta, drain

76

fork and spread it around the dish with your hands so that it moistens the breadcrumbs. Transfer the pasta and tomato to the dish, then cover with a layer of chicken giblets and mushrooms. Cover with the rest of the macaroni in the sauce. Cover the pan with kitchen foil and leave to cook in a preheated oven at 160°C for about one hour. Remove the timbale from the oven and allow to rest for a few minutes before serving.

when al dente, and flavour with some of the meat sauce. Serve the remaining sauce in a sauceboat with a dish of grated Parmesan cheese on the side.

MACARONI TIMBALE

◀ Campania ▶

500 g macaroni (or other short type of pasta, i.e. rigatoni), 500 g ripe, firm tomatoes, 300 g chicken giblets, 30 g dried mushrooms, 1 egg, breadcrumbs, extra-virgin olive oil, salt, pepper.

Steep the mushrooms in lukewarm water. Skin the tomatoes, remove the seeds and chop. Clean the giblets. Cook the giblets whole or sliced into large pieces in a little oil with the drained, dried and chopped mushrooms. Add the chopped tomatoes. Add salt and pepper and allow the sauce to thicken over a rapid heat. Meanwhile cook the pasta in plentiful salt water, drain when half-cooked. Mix the pasta in tomato sauce, leaving aside the mushrooms and giblets.
Grease a baking dish (preferably of a truncated cone shape) and sprinkle with bread crumbs. Beat the egg with a

TORTELLINI IN BROTH

◀ Veneto ▶

400 g flour, 4 eggs, 1 litre meat stock, salt.
For the filling: 100 g chicken breast, 200 g pork loin, 1 small salami, chicken livers and gizzards (optional), 150 g grated Parmesan cheese, nutmeg, breadcrumbs, salt, pepper.

In a pot place the chopped chicken and pork, the skinned and chopped salami and if desired, also the liv-

77

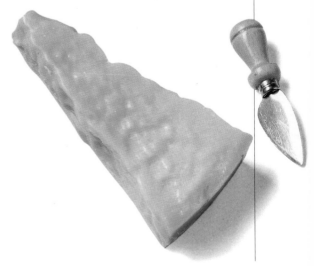

PUMPKIN *TORTELLINI*

◀ *Lombardy* ▶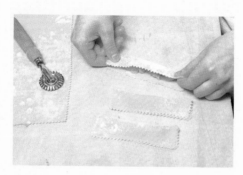

For the pastry: 400 g flour, 4 eggs, salt.
For the filling: 1 kg yellow pumpkin, 100 g macaroons, 150 g grated Parmesan. 1 egg, nutmeg, salt.
For the sauce: sage, butter, grated Parmesan cheese

◆ Scoop out the flesh from the pumpkin, remove the seeds and bake in the oven. Mash the pulp and mix with the beaten egg. Crumble in the macaroons and the Parmesan cheese and season with salt and nutmeg.

◆ Knead together all the ingredients for the pasta, working until you obtain a soft dough with a glossy surface.

◆ Flour the work surface and with a rolling pin and/or a pasta-making machine, roll out the pasta very thinly and cut out some small squares. Drop some of the pumpkin filling into the centre of each square.

◆ Fold over the dough, pressing the edges down well. Cook the tortellini in plentiful salt water, drain and serve flavoured with the melted butter and sage. Accompany with grated Parmesan.
Another version uses Cremona sweet pickle (about 100g), chopped finely and softened in its own juice.

ers and gizzards. Pour the stock or salt water over the meats and allow to boil slowly. After about two hours remove the meat and mince it.

Grate the cheese roughly, add the breadcrumbs with a pinch of nutmeg, salt and pepper. Add just enough stock to bind the ingredients together. Stir until all the ingredients are well mixed and leave to rest at room temperature for a couple of hours to blend the flavours.

Meanwhile prepare the pasta: knead the flour together with the eggs and a pinch of salt, working until you obtain a firm dough with a glossy surface. Sprinkle the work surface with flour and with a rolling pin or a pasta-making machine, roll out to a very thin sheet of pasta, cut into 4 cm squares. In the centre of each drop a little filling, fold over in a triangle and wrap it around your finger, pressing down the ends to seal them. The tortellini are cooked and served in the best quality meat broth.

TRENETTE WITH PESTO
◀ Liguria ▶ 📷

400 g trenette, 30 basil leaves, 1 clove of garlic, 1-2 dessertspoons pine-nuts, 1 dessertspoon grated pecorino, 1 dessertspoon grated Parmesan, extra-virgin olive oil, salt.

Wash the basil leaves and crush them in a stone mortar together with the garlic and pine-nuts (using a circular movement against the sides of the mortar) Add the grated cheeses and a pinch of salt. As soon as you have obtained a smooth mixture, dilute with just enough oil to obtain a creamy substance which is not too runny. The sauce can also be made in a blender. Cook the trenette in plentiful salt water, drain and flavour with the pesto to which has been added two dessertspoons of the pasta cooking water.

The traditional Ligurian recipe also allows for trofie to be used instead of trenette: this is a small curly pasta like corkscrews. The recipe is as follows.

TROFIE
◀ Liguria ▶

400 g of white flour, water, salt.

Put the flour and salt into a bowl with a pinch of salt, then add as much water as required.

Mix thoroughly in the bowl, then turn out onto a floured surface and knead well until you have a smooth, springy dough. Break off pieces about the size of a bean, roll them into thin sausages then, with well-floured hands, twist them into corkscrew shapes. Leave them to dry on a flour-sprinkled tea-cloth for four hours, then cook and serve with pesto or one of the following sauces:

Tomato and olive sauce
100 g black olives, 3 ripe firm tomatoes, 1 sprig parsley, 1 sprig basil, 1 leek, grated pecorino cheese, 1 glass dry white wine, extra-virgin olive oil, salt, pepper.

Cook the chopped parsley and leek in the oil until golden. Add the tomatoes, peeled and cut into strips, the stoned, sliced olives and a little salt. Pour over

the white wine, then let it evaporate, cooking over a low heat. Cook the trofie in plenty of boiling salted water, drain them while they are still al dente, and tip into the pan with the sauce.

Sauté for a couple of minutes, blending in the sauce, then add the finely chopped basil, a sprinkle of grated pecorino, a grind of pepper, and serve immediately.

Anchovy sauce

4 anchovy fillets, 1 ripe tomato, 1 onion, 1 sprig basil, 1/2 red chilli, 1 glass dry white wine, extra-virgin olive oil.

Mash the anchovies with a fork. Chop the onion and chilli and cook in the oil until golden. Add the anchovies, pour in the white wine, and let it evaporate. Peel the tomato, cut in strips, and leave to one side. Cook the trofie in plenty of salted water, drain them and tip them into a bowl. Add the anchovy sauce, the tomato, a trickle of oil and the chopped basil. Mix thoroughly, and serve.

VINCISGRASSI

◀ Marche ▶

For the pasta: 400 g flour, 200 g semolina, 5 eggs, 40 g butter, Vinsanto (sweet wine), salt.
For the béchamel sauce: 60 g butter, 50 g flour, 6 dl milk, grated nutmeg, salt, pepper.
For the meat sauce: 100 g bacon fat, 1 small onion, 300 g chicken giblets, 450 g calves' sweetbreads and bone marrow, white wine, 250 g tomato pulp, 200 g Parmesan cheese, nutmeg, stock as required, extra-virgin olive oil, salt, pepper.

Put the flour, semolina, eggs, melted but-

ter, a pinch of salt and a finger of Vinsanto into a bowl. Mix and knead well, then set aside for at least half an hour. Roll out the pasta and cut into 10x15 cm sheets. Boil in plenty of salted water, and when they are half-cooked, drain the sheets and lay them out to cool on a clean cloth. To prepare the meat sauce: fry the chopped onion and the bacon fat in oil, add the finely-chopped chicken giblets, brown for a few minutes then pour on the white wine. As soon as it has evaporated, add the tomato pulp, salt, pepper and a pinch of grated nutmeg. Cook for about fifteen minutes, then add the diced bone marrow and sweetbreads, and salt to taste. Cover the pan and leave to boil for about an hour and a half, adding hot stock during cooking if necessary. Meanwhile prepare the béchamel: melt the butter over a low heat, and add the flour. Stir in the hot milk a little at a time, mixing all the time. After the sauce begins to boil, continue cooking for ten minutes, stirring constantly, then season with salt, pepper and a pinch of nutmeg before switching off the heat. Butter an ovenproof dish and arrange alternate layers of pasta, béchamel sauce, grated parmesan, meat sauce and a few knobs of butter. Finish up with a layer of pasta covered with béchamel and grated parmesan. Cook in a pre-heated oven for about 30-40 minutes.

CHICKPEA SOUP

◀ Marche ▶

250 g chickpeas, 1 onion, 2 celery stalks, 3 tomatoes, 1 carrot, a few chard leaves, 2 cloves

garlic, grated pecorino cheese, extra-virgin olive oil, salt, toasted bread.

Leave the chickpeas to steep for 24 hours, then drain. Slice the onion and chard, chop the celery and the carrot, crush the garlic, dice the tomatoes and put them all into a pot with the chickpeas. Add about 1.5 litres of water and cook for about two hours, then season with salt and oil. Place some toasted bread in each plate, pour the soup over, and sprinkle with pecorino cheese.

BROAD BEAN AND CHICORY SOUP

◄ Puglia ►

6 cups freshly podded broad beans, 2 small heads of chicory, 2 onions, basil, extra-virgin olive oil, salt.

Boil the broad beans in 1.5 litres of water, drain them and retain the cooking water, then pass half the beans through a food mill. Wash the chicory, then blanch it in the bean cooking water, and chop it. Wash and slice the onions, then put them in a saucepan and sauté them in oil for a few minutes. Add the puréed beans, and some of the cooking water, and then the whole broad beans. Bring to the boil then take off the heat. Season with oil and garnish with basil.

MAIZE SOUP

◄ Friuli Venezia Giulia ►

250 g dry beans, 250 g maize, 1 carrot, 1

onion, 1 celery stalk, 50 g lard, salt, freshly ground pepper.

Steep the beans in warm water overnight, then drain them and boil them in fresh water with the maize for about two hours; add salt towards the end of cooking. Prepare a base of finely-chopped carrot, onion and celery sautéed in lard, and add it to the soup. Leave to cook for a few more minutes then turn off the heat. Serve the soup piping hot, with freshly ground pepper.

GOULASH SOUP

◄ Trentino-Alto Adige ►

1 litre meat stock, 400 g lean beef, 1 large onion, 1 large potato, 1 clove garlic, 400 g peeled chopped tomatoes (optional), 2 teaspoons paprika, 1/2 teaspoon cumin powder, 3 dessertspoons flour, 6 teaspoons extra-virgin olive oil, salt, pepper.

Heat the oil in a large pot, add the meat cut into small half-centimetre cubes and the thinly-sliced onion. Cook over a moderate heat for about 4-6 minutes until the meat and onion are golden. Add the crushed garlic, cumin, paprika and flour and sauté for another minute. Add the stock gradually and then bring to the boil, cover, and cook over a moderate heat for 2 hours. Dice the potato and add it to the soup with the tomatoes, then season with salt and pepper. Cook for another thirty minutes until the potatoes are soft, then serve.

BARLEY SOUP

◄ *Trentino-Alto Adige* ►

300 g barley, 150 g dried beans, 1 ham bone, 2 potatoes, 2 carrots, 1 onion, 1 celery stalk, a sprig of parsley, grated Parmesan cheese, extra-virgin olive oil, salt.

In two different containers, steep the ham bone and the beans overnight (12 hours). Then drain the beans, add fresh water and cook over a low heat for about 2 hours.
Steep the barley for 24 hours, then rinse it under running water. Cover with fresh water and boil this too for about 2 hours. Slice the onion finely and wash and chop the parsley, then sauté lightly in oil. Add this mixture to the barley when it has just begun to boil, along with the sliced potatoes and carrots, the drained ham bone and salt and hot water as required. At the end of cooking, add the boiled beans and remove the ham bone. Serve the soup with grated grana cheese.

CELERY SOUP

◄ *Calabria* ►

600 g celery, 200 g sausage, 200 g caciocavallo cheese, 3 eggs, grated pecorino cheese, extra-virgin olive oil, salt, pepper, toasted bread.

Wash and chop the celery and set it to cook in a saucepan with 1.5 litres of water, salt, pepper and a few dessertspoons of oil. Let it simmer slowly until the celery has softened. Chop up the sausage, and dice the caciocavallo, hard-boil the eggs, shell them and cut into wedges. Place all these ingredients on top of toasted slices of bread in a tureen, pour the celery soup over them, garnish with grated pecorino cheese and serve piping hot.

SPICY MEAT SOUP

◄ *Campania* ►

1 kg pork offal (heart, spleen and lungs), 1.5 litres meat stock, 1 glass red wine, rosemary, tomato purée, 30 g lard, extra-virgin olive oil, salt, chilli, pepper, toasted bread.

Steep the pork offal for about an hour. Heat equal quantities of lard and oil in a saucepan, then brown the chopped offal lightly. Pour over the red wine, and let it evaporate. Cover completely with the tomato purée, and season with salt, pepper, chilli and rosemary. Gradually ladle in the boiling meat stock, and cook over a low heat for about an hour. Serve the soup hot, poured over the toasted bread.

MEAT
DISHES

ROAST SPRING LAMB WITH POTATOES

◄ Lazio ►

1 kg (generous) leg and shoulder spring lamb, 70 g lean and fat ham, 1 kg potatoes, garlic, rosemary, bay leaves, 1/2 glass dry white wine, lard, extra-virgin olive oil, salt pepper.

Cut slits in the lamb with a long fine-bladed knife, and fill them with pieces of garlic, small sprigs of rosemary and fat and lean bits of ham. Then spread it with lard, and season with salt and pepper. Place it in a roasting tin, with oil and a few bay leaves. Arrange the peeled potatoes around the meat, seasoning them with salt, pepper and a trickle of oil. Place in a pre-heated oven, and after about half an hour sprinkle the lamb with the white wine. During cooking, turn the potatoes and the lamb over from time to time so that they don't stick to the tin. Leave to cook for another 30 minutes, and when all is well browned, remove from the oven. Cut the meat into pieces, and serve.

ROAST LAMB WITH "MENTUCCIA" MINT

◄ Abruzzo-Molise ►

1.8 kg leg of lamb, 1 onion, 1 carrot, 1 celery stalk, 3 cloves garlic, 1 bunch "mentuccia" mint, 1/2 glass extra-virgin olive oil, salt, pepper.

With a suitably sharp knife, bone the lamb, and remove the leg bone. Spread the meat with a finely-chopped mix-ture of the garlic and half the mint, then sprinkle with salt and pepper. Roll up the meat tie it with string like a roast, then rub with salt and pepper. Place it in a good-sized roasting-tin, season it with a roughly-chopped mixture of celery, carrot, onion and garlic, and sprinkle it with oil. Cook in a pre-heated oven for about an hour and a half. Turn the lamb over from time to time, basting it with the juices, to give it an even, golden colour. Add the rest of the chopped mint just a few minutes before you remove from the oven. Serve the lamb at table, along with the strained cooking juices.

LAMB IN *POTACCHIO*

◄ Marche ►

800 g lamb, 300 g ripe firm tomatoes, 1 spoon tomato purée, 1 small onion, 1 clove garlic, 1 sprig rosemary, dry white wine, extra-virgin olive oil, salt, pepper

Sauté the finely chopped onion, garlic and rosemary in a few spoons of oil in an earthenware pot. As soon as it begins to brown, add the lamb cut into chunks. Brown it all over, then season with salt and chilli pepper. Pour over white wine to taste, and as soon as it has almost evaporated, add the tomato purée diluted with a little water, and the peeled, seeded and chopped tomatoes. Cover, and cook the meat thoroughly over a moderate heat.
This method of stewing in potacchio can also be used for other types of meat (chicken, rabbit etc.)

FLORENTINE BEEFSTEAK

◀ *Tuscany* ▶

1 600 g T-bone steak for every two guests, extra-virgin olive oil, salt, pepper

For the famous Florentine style steak it's essential to use young beef. The cut should include both the fillet and the sirloin, and be about 2 cm thick. Put the steaks on the grill, preferably over a charcoal fire. Cook for 5-6 minutes on each side, then sprinkle with salt and pepper. Leave on the fire for another minute, then serve immediately with a trickle of extra-virgin olive oil.

MIXED BOILED MEAT

◀ *Valle d'Aosta-Piedmont* ▶

1 kg beef, 1 free-range pullet, 500 g calf's head, 500 g pickled tongue, 1 cotechino (spiced pork sausage), 2 onions, 2 carrots, 1 celery stalk, salt.

Place the pullet, the beef and the chopped vegetables into a large pot. Add water and salt, bring to the boil, and simmer on a low heat for 2 hours, skimming every so often. Cook the tongue, the calf's head, and the cotechino, each separately. Serve the meat very hot, sliced. Traditionally the boiled meat is served accompanied by the following recommended sauces.

Red sauce
4 large very ripe tomatoes, 1/2 pepper, 1/2 celery stalk, 1 onion, 1 clove garlic, 1 sprig basil, 1 sprig parsley, 1 sprig rosemary, 1 chilli pepper, extra-virgin olive oil, salt.

Peel and chop the tomatoes and sauté them in the oil with the finely chopped

87

vegetables, the herbs and a pinch of salt. Once cooked, pass through a sieve or a food-mill and bring to the boil again. Take it off the heat and add a trickle of olive oil.

Green sauce

1 bunch parsley, 2 eggs, 2 anchovy fillets, 8 capers, bread (without crust), 1 clove garlic, vinegar, extra-virgin olive oil, salt.

Finely chop the parsley, garlic, hard-boiled egg yolks, anchovy fillets, capers and the bread soaked in vinegar. Blend the ingredients well, adding salt and enough oil to make a fine, smooth sauce.

POT ROAST WITH *BAROLO*

◀ *Valle d'Aosta-Piedmont* ▶

1.5 kg beef, 1 piece Parma ham fat, 2 onions, 2 carrots, 1 celery stalk, 1 bay leaf, 2-3 sage leaves, 1 sprig rosemary, 3 glasses Barolo wine, extra-virgin olive oil, salt, pepper.

Brown the beef in olive oil, along with the diced ham fat. Pour over the wine, and turn down the heat. Add the chopped onions, carrots and celery, and then the bay leaf, sage and rosemary. Season with salt and pepper, and add a few glasses of water. Simmer over a low heat for about two hours. Slice the meat, and serve it with the sieved cooking juices.

ROAST KID

◀ Sardinia ▶

2 pieces of kid (shoulder and back), 2 cloves garlic, 1 bunch parsley, a few basil leaves, a few myrtle leaves, 2 slices fatty bacon, 1 dessertspoon breadcrumbs, extra-virgin olive oil, salt, pepper.

Sprinkle the pieces of kid with salt and pepper, then wrap them with the slices of bacon. Place them in an oiled roasting tin, and cook in a pre-heated oven at moderate temperature for about half an hour. Turn the meat over every so often, basting it with the cooking juices.

Meanwhile, peel the garlic and wash and dry the parsley, then chop them finely and mix with the breadcrumbs. Remove the tin from the oven, spread the bread and herb mixture over the meat, and return to the oven for a few minutes, turning the heat up to brown the meat. Serve piping hot.

STEWED VENISON

◀ Trentino-Alto Adige ▶

1 kg venison, 50g bacon, 5-6 bay leaves, red wine, stock as required, extra-virgin olive oil, salt, pepper.

For the marinade: 1 litre red wine, 5-6 sage leaves, 2-3 sprigs rosemary, thyme, 3-4 cloves.

Steep the venison in red wine seasoned with the sage, rosemary, cloves and a few sprigs of thyme. Leave to marinate for 24 hours. Then chop the bacon and put it into a saucepan with a little oil and a knob of butter. Drain the meat of its marinade, chop it into pieces, and brown it with the bacon. Add salt and pepper, and sprinkle with red wine. Pour over a ladleful of stock together with the bay leaves. Cook slowly for about two hours, adding more stock if required.

STUFFED BREAST OF VEAL

◀ Liguria ▶ 📷

700 g breast of veal, 100 g sweetbreads, 100 g ham, 100 g bread (without crust), 25 g pistachios, 25 g pine-nuts, 2 artichokes, 50 g peas, 1/2 onion, 1 carrot, 1 celery stalk, 1 clove garlic, 1 sprig marjoram, 1 bay leaf, 2 basil leaves, nutmeg, 2 eggs, 1 cup milk, grated pecorino cheese, extra-virgin olive oil, salt, pepper.

Ask the butcher to bone the breast and prepare it in the form of a pocket.

Par-boil the meat and the sweetbreads in plenty of boiling water. Steep the bread in milk, then squeeze it and set aside. Sauté the finely-chopped onion in oil, add the peas, the diced ham, the sweetbreads, the pistachios, the pine-nuts, the chopped artichoke hearts and the soaked bread. Season with a pinch of grated nutmeg, the chopped basil and marjoram, the grated pecorino and salt, and take off the heat. Beat the eggs, add to the other ingredients and mix well until thoroughly blended.

Stuff the pocket of the veal with this mixture. Sew up the opening. Wrap it up in cheesecloth, tied at both ends, and place it in a pan of boiling salted water with the chopped onion, celery and carrot and the bay leaf. Boil for two hours, then remove from the stock and place it on a wooden board to cool.

To serve, remove the cloth, slice the stuffed veal and bring to the table garnished with sprigs of parsley.

CINGHIALE ALLA CACCIATORA

◀ Sardinia ▶

1 kg wild boar, 100 g thinly sliced Parma ham, 1 onion, celery, parsley, vinegar, 1 glass white wine, meat stock as required, butter, salt, pepper.

Steep the meat in the vinegar for at least half an hour. Drain it, wrap with the slices of ham, and tie with string. Melt the butter in a saucepan and brown the meat. Season with salt and pepper and continue cooking, turning every so often. Add the roughly chopped celery and onion, a sprig of parsley, the white wine and meat stock. Simmer for about an hour over a low heat, then reduce the cooking juices before serving.

BRAISED OXTAIL

◀ Lazio ▶

1 kg oxtail, 1 small piece ox cheek, 200 g firm ripe tomatoes, 1 onion, 1 carrot, 1 celery stalk, 1 clove garlic, 1 handful pine-nuts, 50 g lard, 1/2 glass red wine, 1/2 glass extra-virgin olive oil, salt, pepper.

Place a knob of lard in a pot and sauté the finely-chopped onion, carrot and garlic and a little parsley. Add the washed and chopped oxtail and cheek, season with salt and pepper and pour over the wine. Brown the meat evenly, then add the peeled, seeded and chopped tomatoes. Cover, and continue cooking over a very low heat for about 4-5 hours, adding a few ladlefuls of hot salted water if the sauce should become too dry. When the meat is tender enough to fall off the bone, add the celery, washed and cut into finger-length sticks, and finally the pine-nuts. Cook for a further 20 minutes, then serve piping hot. The more traditional version of this recipe also includes a pinch of cocoa powder.

ROAST RABBIT

◀ Liguria ▶

1 rabbit (1 kg or over), 100 g ham, 100 g pork, 100 g fresh bacon rind, 1 milk bread roll, 1

onion, 1 carrot, 1 celery stalk, 1-2 cloves garlic, fennel leaves, thyme, rosemary, 1 dl white wine, 1/2 glass extra-virgin olive oil, salt, pepper.

Wash the rabbit, chop it into pieces and sauté in extra-virgin olive oil together with the chopped onion, the whole cloves of garlic, the rosemary and a pinch of oregano. When the meat is browned, season with salt and pepper and pour over the white wine. When this has evaporated, add a few spoonfuls of stock, cover the saucepan and cook slowly. Turn over the pieces of meat every so often, adding extra stock if required. Just before removing from the heat, add a handful of black, stoned olives. Mix well and serve.

RABBIT IN *PORCHETTA*

◀ *Umbria* ▶

1 rabbit (about 1 kg, complete with liver), 100 g ham, 100 g pork, 100 g fresh bacon rind, 1 milk bread roll, 1 onion, 1 carrot, 1 celery stalk, 1-2 cloves garlic, fennel leaves, thyme, rosemary, 1 dl

white wine, 1/2 glass extra-virgin olive oil, salt, pepper.

Take the rabbit liver, the ham, the pork, the bacon rinds, the garlic and the fennel leaves, chop them all finely and mix well together, seasoning with salt and pepper. Leave the mixture for a few minutes to let the flavours blend.
In the meantime clean the rabbit and wash it thoroughly under running water. Dry it, rub the inside with salt and pepper, and fill with the meat stuffing. Sew up with kitchen thread, and place it in an oiled roasting-tin. Brown the meat evenly in a pre-heated oven, then add the roughly-chopped carrot, onion and celery. Continue cooking for about an hour, turning the rabbit every so often, and basting with the cooking juices. About ten minutes before you turn off the oven, pour over the wine, letting it dry. Serve the rabbit accompanied by the stuffing and the sieved cooking juices.

91

COTECHINO

◀ *Emilia Romagna* ▶

1 Cotechino (spiced pork sausage) of about 1 kg.

Before cooking, pierce the cotechino with a fork or a toothpick, then wrap it up in cheesecloth, tying it at both ends and all along its length.
Fill a large pot with cold water and immerse the sausage. Bring it to the boil, then lower the flame and leave it to simmer for about 3 hours. Test it every so often with a fork to see if it is

cooked, and when it is, turn off the heat and leave the sausage in the water for another 10 minutes. Remove from the pot, cut fairly thick slices, and serve it steaming hot. It goes well with potato purée, spinach cooked in butter with parmesan cheese, and with boiled lentils or beans.

PHEASANT WITH MUSHROOMS AND ONIONS

◀ *Valle d'Aosta-Piedmont* ▶

1 pheasant, 200 g fresh mushrooms, 12 flat white onions, 100 g bacon, 1/2 glass cognac, stock as required, 100 g butter, salt, pepper, toasted bread.

Pluck and clean the pheasant, cut it into four parts, and wrap these in strips of bacon. Place the butter in a pot and brown the meat on both sides. Add the cognac and, when it has evaporated, a ladleful of stock. Continue cooking, seasoning with salt and pepper, and adding more stock if required.
Boil the onions to the point where they are still firm, clean and slice the mushrooms, and add both to the pheasant 20 minutes before the end of cooking. Serve with toasted bread.

FALSOMAGRO

◀ *Sicily* ▶

800 g slice of beef, 150 g lean minced pork, 2 sausages, 3 slices bacon, 2 eggs, 1 onion, 1 clove garlic, 50 g fresh pecorino cheese, red wine, stock as required, extra-virgin olive oil, salt, pepper.

Boil the eggs for 8 minutes, then shell them. Prepare the stuffing for the roast

by mixing the minced pork with the skinned sausages. Sauté for 10 minutes in a small quantity of oil, adding half a sliced onion. Lay out the slice of beef, and spread the sautéed meat over it. Spread over this the slices of bacon, the sliced hard-boiled eggs, the pecorino cheese in flakes and the garlic chopped fine. Salt lightly and dust with pepper. Then roll it up and tie it with string. Put some oil and the rest of the sliced onion in a pot, and brown the stuffed roast all over. Pour over a glass of red wine and let it evaporate, then lower the heat, and continue to cook for about an hour, adding the stock a little at a time.

LIVER, VENETIAN STYLE

◀ *Veneto* ▶ 📷

700 g calves' liver, 700 g white onions, milk or vinegar, parsley, butter, extra-virgin olive oil, salt.

Cut the liver into strips and leave it to marinate in the milk (or in vinegar and water) for at least an hour.
Slice the onions finely and sauté them very slowly in butter and oil. Drain the liver strips and add them to the onions and cook them over a very high heat. Season with salt towards the end of cooking, sprinkle with chopped parsley, and serve.

FINANZIERA

◀ *Valle d'Aosta-Piedmont* ▶

100 g mincemeat, 100 g veal fillet, 100 g bone marrow, 100 g brains, 100 g neck sweetbreads (or sweetbreads), 50 g chicken liver, 50 g pig's

liver, 50 g cocks' combs, 50 g sweetbreads, 50 g kidney, 50 g shelled peas, 100 g porcini mushrooms in oil, 60 g butter, 1 glass Barolo wine, 1 cup stock, 1 dessertspoon vinegar, 2 dessertspoons Marsala, flour, salt, pepper.

Cut the veal fillet in strips and the kidneys into chunks and brown them in the butter, adding a little stock and a pinch of salt and pepper. Separately, make balls from the mincemeat, and cut the bone marrow into pieces of about 3 cm. Chop up the brain, the liver, the sweetbreads, the chicken livers, the pig's liver and the cocks' combs. Dust all the meat with flour and sauté it slowly in butter, adding the peas and the thinly-sliced mushrooms at the end.

When they are cooked, combine the two meat mixtures, pour over the Barolo and let it evaporate. Shortly before serving, sprinkle with the vinegar and the Marsala, and present on an attractive serving-dish.

FONDUE

◀ Valle d'Aosta-Piedmont ▶

300 g fontina cheese, 4 eggs, milk as required, 50 g butter, salt, freshly ground pepper, toasted bread.

Dice the Fontina, then cover it with milk and leave overnight. The next day, melt the butter with a little milk and the Fontina in a double saucepan, stirring continually so that the cheese is completely melted.

Take it off the heat, and add the egg yolks one by one, season with salt and plenty of freshly-ground pepper. Put it back to cook in the bain-marie, stirring constantly, and not letting it boil. When you have a smooth, dense cream, turn off the heat, and serve the fondue on warm plates with lightly toasted slices of bread.

MIXED FRY, PIEDMONT STYLE

◀ Valle d'Aosta-Piedmont ▶

300 g sausage, 300 g liver, 300 g lung, 300 g veal fillet, 100 g brains, 2 apples, 6 carrots, 3 potatoes, 6 macaroons, 200 g semolina, 1/2 litre milk, 100 g sugar, grated lemon peel, 2 eggs, breadcrumbs, flour, olive oil, salt.

Prepare all the ingredients for the mixed fry. Over a low heat, amalgamate the semolina with the milk, sugar and lemon peel, and stir until you have a rich, creamy paste. Turn this out onto a marble slab and leave to cool, then cut into lozenge shapes. Cut the sausage up and brown in a little oil.

Clean the brain, the liver and the lung, and cut into slices. Peel and slice the apples and potatoes, and slice the carrots.

When all the ingredients are ready, coat them all, including the macaroons, by dipping them in flour, beaten egg and then breadcrumbs, and then fry them in boiling oil. Remove excess oil by laying them on absorbent kitchen paper, sprinkle with salt, and serve piping hot.

GOULASH
◀ Friuli Venezia Giulia ▶

800 g shin beef, 2 large onions, 2 cloves garlic, 2 dessertspoons paprika, 1 bay leaf, 1 teaspoon cumin seeds, 1/2 teaspoon marjoram leaves, 1 lemon, 1 glass red wine, 1 glass wine vinegar, 4 dessertspoons lard, 1 dessertspoon butter, salt.

Heat the lard in a heavy-bottomed pan, add the onions cut in thin rings and sauté them until golden. Gather them to the side of the pan, and in the free space sauté the meat cut into fairly small pieces. Mix the two together and continue to brown until a thin golden crust is formed on the bottom of the pan. Pour over the wine and the vinegar, and wait until some of the liquid has evaporated. Then season with salt, dust with paprika, add a glass of water, and leave to stew over a moderate heat for about an hour and a half. Chop the seasonings finely, mix with softened butter and add to the stew together with the juice and peel of the lemon. Allow the flavours to blend for a few minutes before serving.

LEPRE ALLA CACCIATORA
◀ Umbria ▶

1 hare, 50 g fat and lean ham, 1 onion, 2 anchovies, rosemary, capers, 1/2 glass white wine, vinegar, extra-virgin olive oil, salt, pepper, red chilli pepper.

Clean the hare, cut it into pieces and wash it in vinegar. Then put it into a non-stick pan and dry it over a low heat without any other ingredients. Put the oil into a casserole and sauté the finely chopped onion and ham, add the pieces of hare, and season with pepper and salt. While the meat is browning, finely chop the boned anchovies, the rosemary leaves and two dessertspoons of capers. Add this mixture to the hare, diluting it with the white wine and a little oil, and flavouring with a pinch of chilli. When the wine has evaporated, cover the pan, and simmer over a low heat for about 2 hours.

SWEET AND SOUR HARE
◀ Friuli Venezia Giulia ▶

1 hare, 100 g bacon, 1 onion, 2 carrots, 400 g tomatoes, 1/2 lemon, 1 dessertspoon sugar, cinnamon, 1 handful pine-nuts, raisins, maize meal, 1/2 glass red wine, stock as required, extra-virgin olive oil, salt, pepper.

Clean the hare, cut it into pieces, and sauté it in a little oil with the diced bacon and the chopped onion and carrots. When it is browned, sprinkle over a generous handful of maize meal, and blend in. Pour over the red wine and, as soon as it has evaporated, add the sugar, the chopped tomatoes, the cinnamon, the pine-nuts, a few raisins (previously soaked for 15 minutes in warm water, and then squeezed out) the grated lemon-peel, salt and pepper. Allow the flavours to blend, then add some stock and continue to cook over a low heat. Serve with a steaming polenta.

ROAST PIGLET

◄ Sardinia ►

1 sucking pig, 100 g lard, a few sprigs myrtle, 1 bunch parsley, salt, freshly ground pepper.

Carefully clean and wash the piglet, take out the entrails, and rub it first with lard inside and out, and then with salt and coarsely-ground black pepper. Put the sprigs of myrtle and parsley inside, then dress it with more myrtle and place it in a large greased roasting-tin. Place in pre-heated oven, and cook for about 2 hours, turning it every so often and basting with the cooking juices.
Finally bring the piglet to the table, with its skin golden and crispy.

VEAL SHANKS, MILANESE STYLE

◄ Lombardy ►

4 veal shanks, 1 onion, white flour, 1 lemon, parsley, 1 clove garlic, 1 salted anchovy, dry white wine, stock or water as required, 150 g butter, salt, pepper.

Dust the veal shanks thoroughly with flour, and sauté them in the butter. Season with salt and pepper and pour over a little dry white wine. When the wine has evaporated, add enough hot stock or water for cooking, bring to the boil, then leave to simmer for about an hour. Chop the parsley, garlic, onion and the washed and boned anchovy finely, and add this to the meat with the finely-grated lemon peel (yellow part only) about ten minutes before you turn off the heat. Allow the flavours to blend for a few minutes, turning over the veal pieces, then serve, ideally accompanied with a saffron-flavoured risotto.

ROAST PAJATA

◄ Lazio ►

800 g pajata (calf intestines), 500 g potatoes, 2 cloves garlic, 2 sprigs rosemary, vinegar, extra-virgin olive oil, salt, red chilli pepper.

Skin the intestines and cut into long strips, then tie them into rings with kitchen thread and sprinkle with vinegar.
Peel the potatoes, cut them into wedges, spread them in a roasting-tin and cover with the sliced garlic, rosemary, salt and chilli pepper. Arrange the intestines over the potatoes, and cook in a pre-heated oven (at 180°) for about 45 minutes. Turn the potatoes every so often, and adjust salt to taste before serving.

HORSEMEAT *PASTISSÀDA*

◀ *Veneto* ▶

1 kg foal meat, 1 kg onions, 1 litre dry red wine, 3 carrots, 2 bay leaves, 4 cloves, paprika, 1 knob of butter, extra-virgin olive oil, salt, pepper.

This typical dish is a very tasty horse-meat stew, which gets better the longer you cook it. Chop the vegetables finely and sauté them in a saucepan with butter and oil. Add the meat chopped into pieces, and continue to brown for a few minutes. Add the wine, the spices, herbs, salt and pepper, and continue cooking over a very low heat. The dish is ready when the meat tends to fall apart and the vegetables have become puréed. Serve accompanied by a steaming polenta, not too firm.

STEWED LAMB

◀ *Abruzzo-Molise* ▶

1.5 kg lamb, 1 onion, 1 bunch herbs (thyme, bay leaves, rosemary, sage etc.) 1 litre tomato purée, 1/2 glass extra-virgin olive oil, salt, chilli powder.

If necessary, bone the lamb, then salt it inside and tie it up with a string like a roast. Rub the surface of the meat with salt, then brown it in a saucepan in heated oil. When the lamb is evenly coloured all over, add the finely-chopped herbs and onion, and season with chilli. Continue to sauté, turning the meat over from time to time, then add the tomato purée. As soon as this begins to boil, turn down the heat and continue to simmer for about two and a half hours, placing a heat-diffuser plate under the pan.

97

The cooking sauce can, if desired be used as a sauce for pasta, serving the meat as a second course. In this case, use more tomato purée.

PIGEONS IN *SALMÌ*

◀ *Umbria* ▶

2 pigeons, 1 onion, 1 carrot, 1 celery stalk, 1 clove garlic, parsley, sage, rosemary, bay leaf, 1 anchovy, white wine, vinegar, extra-virgin olive oil, salt, pepper, bread.

Clean, wash and cut the pigeons into pieces. Put them into a pot with the chopped onion, carrot, celery and parsley, and sauté in a little oil. Add a few sage leaves, some chopped rosemary, the bay leaf and half a glass each of white wine and vinegar. Season with salt and pepper, and leave to cook for about an hour.
Take the pigeon pieces out of the pot, and pass the cooking sauce through a sieve. Then add the boned and chopped anchovy, the crushed garlic clove and a little vinegar. Put the pigeon back into the pot with the sauce, and leave the flavours to blend for a few minutes over a moderate heat. Serve with pieces of fried bread.

STUFFED PIGEONS

◀ *Basilicata* ▶

2 pigeons, 2 large slices Parma ham (not too thin), 1/2 glass white wine, 1 dessertspoon lard. For the stuffing: the pigeons' giblets, 1 egg, 1 clove garlic, rosemary, 2-3 dessertspoons breadcrumbs, extra-virgin olive oil, salt, pepper.

Pluck and clean the pigeons, retaining the giblets, and season these with salt and pepper. Chop up the innards, then mix them with the breadcrumbs, a little finely-chopped rosemary and garlic. Cook in a little oil, and finally, blend in the egg yolk. Mix all the ingredients thoroughly, and add a little salt. Turn off the heat, and leave to cool. Then stuff the pigeons with the filling, sew up the opening, and wrap them up in the slices of Parma ham.
Melt the lard in a roasting-tin over the hot plate, and brown the pigeons evenly all over. Pour over the white wine, and after a few minutes transfer the tin to a pre-heated oven. Turn the meat over from time to time, adding a little hot salted water if necessary. Cooking time varies from 30 to 45 minutes.

POLENTA PASTICCIATA

◀ *Friuli Venezia Giulia* ▶

200 g fine maize meal, 50 g coarse maize meal, 200 g mutton, 1/2 chicken, 300 g sliced boneless pork, 1 pigeon, 2 sausages, 1 onion, 1 carrot, thyme, sage, rosemary, 1 glass red wine, stock as required, milk, 2 dessertspoons flour, vinegar, butter, extra-virgin olive oil, salt.

Start a few days in advance, and set the mutton to marinate in water and vinegar in a cool place. When it's ready, wash it and sauté in oil and butter along with a mixture of finely-chopped onion, carrot, thyme, sage and rosemary. Add all the other meat, pour over the red wine, and leave it to evaporate; then add a glass of stock and continue to simmer over a low heat for about an hour.

In the meantime, prepare a soft polenta with the two grades of maize meal, using water and milk during cooking. When it is cooked, turn it out onto a board, leave to cool and then slice. Oil a roasting-tin and arrange the slices of polenta in it, covering them with the boned and chopped cooked meats. In another saucepan, melt two dessert-spoons of butter, add the flour and mix to a paste. Dilute this with the sieved cooking-juices of the meat, stirring until you have a rich, creamy sauce. Pour this over the meat and the *polenta*. Put in the oven for 10 minutes, and serve.

POLENTA TARAGNA

◀ Lombardy ▶

400 g buckwheat flour, 50 g butter, 300 g of soft melting cheese (fontina or taleggio, or best of all bitto), salt.

First, prepare the polenta with the buckwheat flour (if you prefer you can mix it with maize meal). When it is cooked, take the polenta off the heat, add the butter cut into knobs and the cheese in slices, then return to the heat for a few minutes, stirring well. When

all the ingredients are thoroughly well blended, serve immediately, steaming hot. Alternative versions suggest seasoning the polenta with a little grated truffle at the moment of serving.

CHICKEN IN SPICY SAUCE

◀ Basilicata ▶

1 large chicken, 400 g ripe tomatoes, 1 onion, 2 red chilli peppers, 1/2 glass white wine, 1 sprig basil, extra-virgin olive oil, salt, pepper.

Clean the chicken, wash it and cut it into small pieces. In a pan, lightly sauté the thinly sliced onion in a little oil. Add the chicken, and stirring all the time, brown it for a few minutes. Then pour over the white wine, and let it evaporate. Peel the tomatoes (this is easier if you plunge them into boiling water for a minute), seed them and chop them roughly. Add them to the chicken mixture, seasoning with the crumbled chillis and salt. Mix well, cover the pan, and leave to cook for about an hour over a low heat, stirring every so often. Add the finely chopped basil just before you turn off the heat.

PUCCIA

◀ Valle d'Aosta-Piedmont ▶

300 g maize meal, 1/2 cabbage, 300 g fatty pork, grated Parmesan cheese, salt, freshly ground pepper.

Clean, wash and chop the cabbage, and dice the pork. Place in a saucepan with 1.5 litres of salted water, bring to the boil and cook for half an hour. Then sprinkle in the maize meal and, stirring with a wooden spoon, continue to cook for another 45 minutes.

Serve the polenta steaming, with a sprinkle of grated parmesan cheese and a grind of black pepper.

SALTIMBOCCA ALLA ROMANA

◀ Lazio ▶

12 thin slices veal, 200 g Parma ham, sage, dry white wine, extra-virgin olive oil, salt, pepper.

Season the slices of meat lightly with salt and pepper, place a slice of Parma ham and a leaf of sage on top of each, then roll them up and fasten with a toothpick. Place them in a frying-pan with oil, and begin to brown. Turn, and after a few minutes, pour over a little white wine. Serve the *saltimbocca* with the cooking juices.

ESCALOPES IN BALSAMIC VINEGAR

◀ Emilia Romagna ▶

700 g sliced veal fillet, white flour, 2 dessert-spoons balsamic vinegar, 2 dessertspoons extra-virgin olive oil, 60 g butter, salt, pepper.

Beat thin the slices of veal and dust them lightly with flour. Heat the butter and oil in a large frying-pan, and cook the escalopes for a minute, without browning. Season with salt and pepper and sprinkle with balsamic vinegar. Let this evaporate, and continue cooking, adding a little stock to produce a creamy sauce, which you then serve over the escalopes.

SCOTTIGLIA

◀ Tuscany ▶

800 g mixed meats (veal, chicken, pork, rabbit etc.), 1 onion, 2 cloves garlic, 1 dessertspoon chopped parsley, rosemary, 1/2 glass red wine, 1/2 glass tomato purée. 1 glass extra-virgin olive oil, salt, pepper.

Chop the garlic, onion, a little rosemary and the parsley very finely, and sauté in oil. While these begin to colour, chop all the meat into pieces, and tip into the pan. Season with salt and pepper, and let the flavours blend for a few minutes before adding the red wine. When this has evaporated, pour in the tomato purée, stir well, cover, and cook over a low heat, adding a little stock (stock cubes may be used) if the meat becomes too dry. Place a piece of toasted bread rubbed with garlic in each plate, and serve the scottiglia over it.

ROAST SHIN OF PORK

◀ Trentino-Alto Adige ▶

4 shins of pork, 1 carrot, 1 celery stalk, 2 sprigs rosemary, 2 glasses white wine, 1 glass stock, extra-virgin olive oil, salt.

Place the meat in a roasting-tin with the chopped vegetables, rosemary, oil and salt. On the hot-plate, colour the meat evenly over a rapid heat, pour over a glass of wine, then transfer to the oven, and continue cooking at a moderate heat for at least two hours. Turn the meat every so often, and baste it with the cooking juices, the rest of the wine and the stock. If the pork should be-

come too dry, cover the roasting tin with a sheet of aluminium foil.

MUTTON STEW

◀ *Sardinia* ▶

2 kg mutton shoulder (usually from a "semen-tusa" - a sheep sheared only once), 2 kg new potatoes, 1.5 kg medium-sized white onions, 3 dried tomatoes, 2 celery stalks, 3 small carrots, parsley, sage, bay leaf, rosemary, mint, salt.

Cut the meat into pieces and place it in a large saucepan with 3 litres of water and the roughly chopped vegetables and herbs (carrots, celery, dried tomatoes, parsley, sage, bay leaf, rosemary, mint) and a little salt. Add the potatoes and the onions, bring to the boil over a low heat, and continue simmering for about two hours, until the liquid is reduced to about half, and has formed a tasty sauce with the vegetables and the mutton fat. Without stirring, check that the various ingredients – the meat, potatoes and onions – are all well covered in sauce. Serve the stew piping hot.

UCCELLINI SCAPPATI

◀ *Lombardy* ▶

8 slices pork loin, 8 slices bacon, 8 sage leaves, 80 g butter, salt, pepper.

Make sure the loin is sliced very fine, then beat the slices and sprinkle them with salt and pepper. Spread a slice of bacon and a sage leave on each, then roll them up and secure with a tooth-pick. Melt the butter in a frying-pan, and cook the pork rolls on a high heat,

turning them, for at least half an hour. Do not overcook, as pork loin tends to become hard. Serve the rolls piping hot, with a soft polenta.

VITELLO TONNATO
(BRAISED VEAL WITH TUNA MAYONNAISE)

◀ *Valle d'Aosta-Piedmont* ▶ 📷

1 kg lean veal, 1 carrot, 1 onion, 1 celery stalk, 1 bay leaf, 200 g tuna in oil, 4 anchovy fillets, 2-3 dessertspoons capers, 2 hard-boiled eggs, 1 lemon, 1 dessertspoon vinegar, extra-virgin olive oil, salt.

Boil the veal in salted water with the carrot, onion, celery, bay leaf and vine-gar, simmering for about an hour and a half. When the meat is cooked, leave it to cool in its cooking juice, then drain it and slice thinly. In the mean-time chop very finely by hand (or bet-ter still mix in a blender) the tuna, an-chovies, capers and the yolks of the hard-boiled eggs, blending together with oil, lemon juice and, if necessary, a little stock. Lay the slices of veal on a serving-plate and cover with the sauce. Leave in a cool place for a few hours before serving.

FISH
DISHES

SWORDFISH *AGGHIOTTA*

◀ *Sicily* ▶

1 kg swordfish, 500 g tomato pulp, 1 onion, 1 clove garlic, bay leaves, parsley, salted capers, white wine, white flour, extra-virgin olive oil, salt.

Skin the fish and cut it into slices, dust with flour and fry in plenty of oil in a frying-pan. Then drain, and leave to dry on absorbent paper, seasoning with salt. Put the chopped onion and garlic, some crumbled bay leaves, the tomato pulp, a pinch of salt and a dash of oil in a roasting-tin on the hot plate. Cook for about twenty minutes, then take off the heat and add the slices of fried fish sprinkled with chopped parsley. Add a few capers and a dash of white wine. Cook in a moderate oven for about fifteen minutes before serving.

BACCALÀ ALLA LIVORNESE
(LIVORNO-STYLE SALT COD)

◀ *Tuscany* ▶

1 kg wet stockfish, 500 g ripe firm tomatoes, 1 onion, 2 cloves garlic, parsley, basil, white flour, extra-virgin olive oil, pepper.

What is actually used for this dish is stockfish (dried cod, not the salt cod known as baccalà), but the recipe is better known by this name. Skin and bone the stockfish, cut it into pieces, then dry them carefully and dust with flour. Flavour a little oil with some chopped garlic, and brown the fish on both sides, then leave to cook on a moderate heat, seasoning with a grind of pepper. Meanwhile prepare the tomato sauce. Peel the tomatoes (plunge them in boiling water for a few seconds), seed them and put them through the food-mill. Add these to the finely-chopped onion sautéed in oil. Cook the sauce until the tomato water has evaporated, then add the chopped basil and parsley, pour over the fish, and continue cooking for about half an hour.

BACCALÀ ALLA VICENTINA
(VICENZA-STYLE SALT COD)

◀ *Veneto* ▶ 📷

1 kg softened stockfish, 50 g salted anchovies, 300 g onion, 1 bunch parsley, white flour, milk, extra-virgin olive oil, salt, pepper.

What is actually used for this dish is stockfish (dried cod, not the salt cod known as baccalà), but the recipe is better known by this name. Slice the onion finely and sauté it in a few dessertspoons of oil. As soon as it has softened (it must not brown) add the chopped parsley and the anchovies, with the bones and salt removed. Heat the sauce well, stirring it so that the anchovies blend into the oil, then turn off the heat. Skin and bone the stockfish, cut it into pieces and dust them lightly in flour. Place them in an earthenware pot, pour over the onion sauce, and add equal parts of oil and milk so that the fish is completely covered. Cover, and leave to cook over a low heat for at least three hours, shaking the pot by the handles every so often. Serve with hot polenta.

CACCIUCCO
(LIVORNO FISH SOUP)

◀ *Tuscany* ▶

600 g unboned soup fish, 800 g whole fish (dogfish, monkfish, mullet etc.) 1 kg molluscs (squid, octopus, cuttlefish etc.) 4-5 squills or scampi (one per person), 500 g ripe tomatoes, 1 onion, 1 carrot, 1 celery stalk, 2 cloves garlic, 1 glass red wine, parsley, extra-virgin olive oil, salt, red chilli pepper, bread slices.

Clean all the fish. Wash and finely chop the onion, carrot and celery, and sauté in plenty of oil. As soon as the onion begins to turn golden, add the roughly-chopped octopus and the cuttlefish. Sauté them lightly, then sprinkle with wine. After about 10 minutes, take them out of the pot, and put in the tomatoes – peeled, seeded and diced – the soup fish, and any other heads from the cleaned fish. Pour over a few ladlefuls of stock or boiling water. Cook for about 15-20 minutes, then sieve the fish or pass it through a food-mill, and return to the heat.
At this point, add the previously cooked molluscs, and water or hot stock if required, and season with salt and chilli pepper. Continue cooking for another 20 minutes, then add the remaining fish (the scampi, squid and the whole fish cut in pieces) and continue simmering for a further 20 minutes. Add a generous handful of chopped parsley just before turning off the heat. Serve in bowls, poured over slices of well-toasted bread. A variant on this recipe substitutes a glass of vinegar for the red wine.

STUFFED SQUID

◀ *Friuli Venezia Giulia* ▶

8 cleaned squid, 2 cloves garlic, 1 egg yolk (optional), 1 handful parsley, breadcrumbs, extra-virgin olive oil, salt, pepper.

Clean, wash and dry the squid. Prepare the filling by chopping the squid tentacles finely with the garlic and parsley. Season with salt and pepper, and fry the mixture in the oil where you have previously sautéed a few dessertspoons of breadcrumbs. Mix all together and, once the mixture has cooled you can use an egg yolk to bind it, if you wish. Then stuff the squid sacks with the filling, closing the top of each one with a toothpick. After this, season with salt and oil, and roast on the pre-heated grill pan.

FISH DISHES

110

PIKE IN SAUCE

◀ *Veneto* ▶ 📷

1 pike (about 1 kg), 1 carrot, 1/2 onion, 1 celery stalk, 1 glass white wine, salt, whole peppercorns.
<u>For the sauce</u>: 150 g parsley, 150 g salted anchovies, 150 g capers, extra-virgin olive oil.

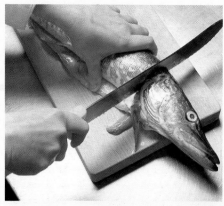

◆ Clean the fish, wash it under running water, and drain well.

◆ In a casserole, boil the fish in water flavoured with the wine and roughly-chopped vegetables, salt and a few peppercorns.

◆ Meanwhile, prepare the sauce: bone the anchovies and remove the salt with a damp cloth, chop them finely with the capers and the parsley, then blend the ingredients together with plenty of oil. When the pike is cooked, bone it and place the fillets in an ovenproof dish.

◆ Spread the sauce over it, and leave to rest for a few hours (preferably overnight) to let the flavours merge. Serve with polenta, either freshly-made or sliced and grilled.

WHITEFISH WITH TOMATOES AND POTATOES

◀ *Lombardy* ▶

2 whitefish of 500 g each, 4 ripe tomatoes, 3 medium-sized potatoes, 4 dessertspoons extra-virgin olive oil, 6 basil leaves, salt, pepper.
<u>For the fish fumet</u>: leftovers of the cleaned fish, 1 carrot, 1 onion, 1 celery stalk, a few bay leaves, 1 bunch parsley, 1 glass white wine, salt.

First, wash the fish carefully, take out the insides, remove the bones and the skin, cut eight fillets and put them aside.
Prepare the fumet by boiling the fish leftovers in water for an hour with the vegetables. Then pass through a sieve and collect the fumet in a frying-pan. Season with salt and add the wine. When the wine is hot, add the white-fish fillets for a few minutes, until the wine has completely evaporated. Then boil the potatoes, peel and dice them, and also dice the peeled tomatoes small. Place the fish on a serving dish with its sauce and cover with the tomatoes, potatoes and chopped basil leaves. Season with salt, pepper and extra-virgin olive oil, and serve.

LAKE WHITEFISH IN FOIL

◀ *Veneto* ▶

4 medium-sized whitefish, 1 onion, 1 celery stalk, 1 carrot, 3 cloves garlic, a few basil leaves, extra-virgin olive oil, salt, pepper.

Clean the fish, wash and dry them, and sprinkle the insides with salt and pepper. Chop the vegetables finely. Prepare a piece of foil for each fish by oiling it and spreading on it a little of the chopped vegetable mixture. Stuff the fish with the rest of the mixture, place each on the prepared foil, and wrap up and seal each packet well. Finally, place in a roasting-tin in a pre-heated oven for 45 minutes.

PANADA ASSEMINESE

◀ *Sardinia* ▶

700 g eels, 300 g semolina, 5 dried tomatoes, 1 sprig parsley, 50 g lard, extra-virgin olive oil, salt, pepper.

Clean the eels, removing the head and the insides, wash and dry them and cut them into pieces. Mix the semolina with a little warm water, the lard (melted in a double saucepan) and a pinch of salt, until you have a soft, elastic dough. Roll this out thin with a rolling pin into two rectangles, one slightly larger than the other. Line a baking-tin with the larger, and then place the eels inside. Chop the parsley, garlic and dried tomatoes finely and spread over the eels, then sprinkle with oil and season with a pinch of salt and a grind of pepper. Cover with the second sheet, pressing up the edges between thumb and forefinger to seal the pie. Cook in a pre-heated oven at a high temperature for thirty minutes, lowering the heat towards the end.

The dried tomatoes can be added in strips, but must in any case be washed and seeded first.

SARDINES A *BECCAFICU*

◀ *Sicily* ▶

1 kg sardines, 5 salted anchovies, 80 g raisins, 80 g pine-nuts, 1 lemon, 1 bunch parsley, 1 bunch basil, a few bay leaves, 2 dessertspoons sugar, 150 g breadcrumbs, extra-virgin olive oil, salt, pepper.

Clean and bone the sardines, splitting them open. Wash them and leave to dry on a tea-cloth.
Remove the salt and any bones from the anchovies and chop them finely. Lightly sauté the breadcrumbs in a few dessertspoons of oil. Steep the raisins in warm water, and then drain. Chop the parsley fine. Mix all these ingredients together, add the pine-nuts, and season with salt and pepper. Spread this mixture over the sardines, roll them up and secure with a toothpick.
Put the sardines into an ovenproof dish with a trickle of oil, alternating them with bay leaves. Make a sauce by dissolving the sugar in the lemon juice and adding a little oil, and pour this over the sardine rolls. Cook in a pre-heated oven at 200°C for about twenty minutes. Serve sprinkled with chopped

basil and accompanied with wedges of lemon.

SCAMPI ALLA BUSARA

◀ *Friuli Venezia Giulia* ▶

12 small prawns, 1 onion, 1 clove garlic, 1 sprig parsley, 1 dessertspoon tomato purée, 1 pinch red chilli powder, 1/2 glass white wine, 1/2 glass extra-virgin olive oil, butter, salt, pepper, toasted bread.

Chop the garlic and onion and sauté in oil in a frying pan. As soon as the onion begins to colour, add the washed and drained prawns. Sauté until the prawns become nice and pink, then pour over the wine and allow this to evaporate over a low heat. At this point, add the chilli, pepper, salt and the tomato purée diluted in half a cup of water. Continue cooking, turning the prawns frequently in the cooking juice. Just before you take the pan off the heat, sprinkle with finely-chopped parsley.
Serve on pieces of toasted bread.

113

TUNA, CATANIA STYLE

◀ *Sicily* ▶

4 slices tuna, 1 crushed clove garlic, 1 cup black olives, 1 cup rinsed capers, 1 cup chopped aromatic herbs, 1 bunch basil, 1 glass white wine, extra-virgin olive oil, chilli, salt.

A dish which is as quick and easy as it is tasty, and a guaranteed success.
Sauté the chopped herbs and the crushed garlic in oil, add the fish, capers and olives, and pour over the wine. Season with a little chilli, then complete the cooking. Serve sprinkled with basil.

VEGETABLE DISHES

ASPARAGUS WITH PARMESAN CHEESE

◀ *Emilia Romagna* ▶

1 kg medium size asparagus, 150 g grated Parmesan cheese, 100 g butter, salt.

Tie the asparagus into bundles with string, and plunge them into a tall pot of boiling water with the tips upwards. The water should come to within a few centimetres of the tips. Cook for about 15 minutes, then take the bundles out and remove the string. Fan out the asparagus in a large frying-pan, with the lower parts of the stems resting on the edge and the tips in the middle. Place on a moderate heat and dot with the butter cut into knobs. When this has melted, sprinkle with about 70 g of grated parmesan, leave to cook for another minute, then turn off the heat.

Arrange the asparagus on a serving-dish in the same way as on the frying-pan, pour the butter left in the pan over the tips, and sprinkle with the remainder of the grated parmesan.

CAPONATA
(SICILIAN STYLE RATATOUILLE)

◀ *Sicily* ▶

4 aubergines, 4 ripe firm tomatoes, 100 g black olives, 1/2 celery stalk, 1 onion, 1 clove garlic, 50g salted capers, cider vinegar, extra-virgin olive oil, coarse salt and table salt.

Clean the aubergines, dice them, cover with coarse salt, and leave them to drip for half an hour in a colander. Meanwhile, slice the onion thinly, crush the garlic, peel the tomatoes (it helps if you plunge them in boiling water for a few seconds), then sieve them or pass them through a food-mill. Stone the olives and chop them roughly, and clean and slice the celery. Put all the ingredients into a pot with a little oil, add the washed capers, and cook over a moderate heat until you have a fairly thick sauce. Drain the water from the aubergines, and sauté them separately in oil before adding to the sauce. Continue cooking for a further ten minutes. Before turning off the heat, adjust salt to taste and add a drop of vinegar. This dish is better served cold.

ARTICHOKES *ALLA GIUDIA*

◀ *Lazio* ▶

4 artichokes, 1 bunch parsley, a few leaves fresh mint, extra-virgin olive oil, salt.

Trim the tops of the artichokes, remove the tough outer leaves, cut off the stems, wash, drain and dry them. Open the central leaves a little and put inside a little chopped mint and parsley and a pinch of salt. Arrange the artichokes standing upright in a small casserole, pour on enough oil to come half way up the sides, and place on the heat. Cook over a high heat without the lid. When the leaves have turned crisp and a deep golden colour, cover the casserole, turn down the heat, and continue cooking for another few minutes. Finally drain the artichokes and arrange them on a serving-dish.

FRIED ARTICHOKES

◀ *Marche* ▶

6 fairly large tender artichokes, 3 eggs, flour, lemon, oil for frying, salt, pepper.

Clean the artichokes, cutting off the stems, the tips and the tough outer leaves. Cut them in wedges and steep them in water mixed with a little lemon juice. Beat the eggs with a pinch of salt and pepper. Dry the artichokes, dust them with flour then dip in the beaten egg and fry rapidly in plenty of boiling oil.

CARDOONS *ALLA BRINDISINA*

◀ *Puglia* ▶

1 kg cardoons, capers, 80 g black olives, 4 boned anchovies, parsley, 1 lemon, breadcrumbs, extra-virgin olive oil, salt, pepper.

Clean the cardoons and cut them into stick-size pieces of equal length. Boil for about an hour in salted water with a dash of lemon

juice. Drain, dry and arrange in layers in a lightly greased oven dish. Sprinkle each layer with capers, stoned olives, the roughly chopped anchovies, chopped parsley, salt and pepper. When the last layer is complete, sprinkle the breadcrumbs over the top and garnish with a trickle of olive oil. Cook in a moderate oven, and remove when it is nicely browned.

SWEET AND SOUR ONIONS

◀ *Emilia Romagna* ▶

450 g small flat white onions, 1/2 glass balsamic vinegar, 40 g sugar, 7 dessertspoons extra-virgin olive oil, 60 g butter, salt.

Peel the onions, and wash and dry them carefully. Then put them in a frying pan over a moderate heat. When they begin to colour, add the butter and oil and sauté, stirring continuously with a wooden spoon. Pour over the vinegar, and let it almost all evaporate, then add the sugar. Lower to minimum heat, cover the frying pan, and continue cooking, adding a little hot water if necessary. After about half an hour, turn the onions over, and continue to cook for a further 30 minutes. When ready, the onions should have produced a sauce which is neither too thick nor too watery. Place the

onions in a serving-dish and pour over the sauce.

SAUERKRAUT

◀ *Trentino Alto Adige* ▶ 📷

1 kg sauerkraut fermented in milk, 3 cloves garlic, stock as required, extra-virgin olive oil, salt.

Heat the oil in a pot, add the crushed cloves of garlic, and sauté lightly, removing from the heat as soon as they begin to colour. Rinse the sauerkraut rapidly under running water, drain, and toss it in the pan with the garlic for a few minutes. Cover with stock or hot water, season with salt, cover, and set it to simmer slowly, stirring every so often.

The success of this dish depends on a slow, patient cooking; it is ready when the cabbage has turned a pale golden colour. Excellent served with frankfurters, it constitutes one of the most typical gastronomic combinations of the cuisine of Alto Adige.

BEANS IN THE FLASK

◀ *Tuscany* ▶ 📷

350 g shelled cannellini beans, 6 sage leaves, 2 cloves garlic, 1/2 glass extra-virgin olive oil, salt, pepper.

This is a traditional recipe, which requires time and patience. First, find an empty glass 2-litre flask. Remove the straw covering, and wash it thoroughly. Fill two-thirds full with the beans, then add the oil, the roughly chopped

sage, the crushed garlic, and two glasses of water. Close the neck of the flask with the leftover straw, or with cotton, but not too tightly so that the water can evaporate during cooking. At this point the Tuscan peasants would place the flask upright in the chimney-place, covering it with warm embers, leaving it to cook slowly for at least 5 hours, or even overnight. In the absence of a fireplace, place the flask in a bain-marie in an ovenproof dish and cook it in the oven at a moderate heat. The beans will be cooked when all the water has evaporated and they have completely absorbed the oil. Pour the beans out of the flask, season with plenty of salt and pepper, and serve them with lashings of extra-virgin olive oil.

BROAD BEANS *ALLA SCAFATA*

◀ *Umbria* ▶

600 g fresh shelled broad beans, 4 large onions, 3 ripe firm tomatoes, 120 g streaky bacon, 1 bunch wild fennel, mint, extra-virgin olive oil, salt, pepper.

Chop up the bacon and the onions and sauté them in the oil in an earthenware pot. As soon as they begin to

brown, add the broad beans and the roughly chopped mint and wild fennel. Sauté for a further five minutes. Peel, seed and chop the tomatoes, then add them to the beans with salt and a grind of pepper. Simmer for about half an hour, adding a few ladlefuls of hot, salted water if required.
(When cooked, the beans should be fairly dry).

CHICKPEA MEAL FRITTERS

◀ *Liguria* ▶

500 g chickpea meal, 1 pinch dried bread yeast, 1 small chopped onion, 1 pinch chopped marjoram, olive oil, salt, pepper.

Gradually blend the chickpea meal with sufficient water to form a thick batter, add the yeast and leave overnight.
Next day, stir in the chopped onion and marjoram, and add a pinch of salt. Drop spoonfuls of the batter into boiling oil and fry rapidly. Serve hot sprinkled with salt.

ORANGE SALAD

◀ *Abruzzo-Molise* ▶

4 sweet oranges, 150 g anchovy fillets in oil, extra-virgin olive oil, salt.

Since this recipe uses un-peeled fruit, it's wise to buy biologically-grown oranges.
Wash the oranges, and cut them in round slices a few millimetres thick. Arrange them on a serving-dish and lay over them the

in cold water, changing it frequently. Drain well, and then cut a cross in the bottom of each onion. Arrange them in a roasting-tin with oil, salt and freshly-ground pepper.

Cook in a moderate oven for about an hour, turning every so often.

anchovy fillets cut in strips.
Dress with a trickle of oil and a sprinkle of salt. Leave aside in a cool place for a while before serving.

BAKED *LAMPASCIONI* (WILD ONIONS)

◀ *Puglia* ▶

500 g fresh lampascioni, extra-virgin olive oil, salt, pepper.

To temper the bitter flavour characteristic of these "wild onions", peel them and leave to steep for two days

BAKED AUBERGINES

◀ *Basilicata* ▶

4 medium-size aubergines, 4 dried tomatoes, 1 clove garlic, 1 bunch parsley, a few basil leaves, extra-virgin olive oil, salt, pepper.

Trim and wash the aubergines, cut them in half lengthwise, sprinkle with salt and weight them down on a sloping surface so that the bitter juice can run off. In the meantime, wash and dry the parsley and basil, peel the garlic and chop all together very finely.
Dry the aubergines on a clean tea cloth, make a few slits in each one with a knife, and fill these with the chopped herb mixture.

Arrange the aubergines with the cut side upwards in an oiled ovenproof dish, spread them with the chopped dried tomatoes, and place in a pre-heated oven at 180° C for at least half an hour. The aubergines are excellent served either hot or cold.

121

STUFFED AUBERGINES

◀ *Puglia* ▶

4 aubergines, 100 g mortadella sausage, 2 ripe firm tomatoes, 2 eggs, breadcrumbs, 1 handful grated pecorino cheese, extra-virgin olive oil, salt, pepper.

Cut the aubergines in half lengthwise and scoop out the central part of the flesh. Chop this up, add the chopped tomatoes and sauté in a little oil with salt and pepper for about twenty minutes. Add the beaten eggs, the pecorino cheese, some breadcrumbs and the chopped mortadella. Mix well and use this filling to stuff the aubergine shells. Arrange them in an oiled ovenproof dish, and sprinkle with cheese, salt and pepper. Pour half an inch of water into the dish and cook in a moderate oven for about an hour.

POTATO PANCAKE

◀ *Friuli Venezia Giulia* ▶

1 kg potatoes, 1 onion, 1 ladleful stock, 2 dessert-spoons lard (or the equivalent of extra-virgin olive oil) salt, pepper.

Boil the potatoes in their skins, leave them to cool a little, then skin them and cut them into thick slices. SautÈ the thinly-sliced onion in the lard (or oil) in a large frying-pan. As soon as it begins to colour, add the potatoes, salt, pepper and the stock. Press the potatoes against the bottom of the pan with a wooden spoon or a fork, then let them roast over a slow heat until they form a golden crust on the bottom of the pan. Turn over the potato pancake and brown it in the same way on the other side.

If you have the time and patience you can continue turning the potato cake over, making sure you incorporate all the crust each time. The end result will be even more crisp and tasty.

PEPERONATA

◀ *Puglia* ▶

500 g red and yellow peppers, 2 large onions, 400 g tomatoes, basil, 2 dessertspoons capers, 1 pinch oregano, extra-virgin olive oil, salt, pepper.

Char the peppers over a flame or under the grill, then peel off the skin. Open them, remove the seeds and cut in thin strips. Peel the tomatoes (this is easier

if you plunge them in boiling water for a few seconds) and chop them small. Slice the onions and sauté in a saucepan with a little oil. Add the peppers, tomatoes, capers, a few leaves of basil, a pinch of oregano and finally the salt and pepper. Cook over a low heat for about forty-five minutes, stirring every so often. The peperonata can be served either hot or cold.

PEPPERS WITH BREADCRUMBS

◀ *Calabria* ▶

1 kg peppers, 1 dessertspoon salted capers, oregano, 1 dessertspoon soft breadcrumbs, 2 dessertspoons grated pecorino, 1/2 glass extra-virgin olive oil, salt, chilli pepper.

Remove the seeds and white inner parts of the peppers, then wash them and cut them lengthwise into large wedges. Heat the oil in a large saucepan and sauté the peppers for a few minutes. If you wish, you can then eliminate some of the oil. Add to the peppers the breadcrumbs mixed with the grated cheese, the capers, a pinch of oregano, salt and chilli pepper. Before serving, leave to cook for another few minutes, mixing with a wooden spoon, to allow the flavours of the various ingredients to blend.

PEAS WITH PARMA HAM

◀ *Lazio* ▶

1 kg fresh peas, 1 onion, 150 g Parma ham, 1 sprig parsley, stock as required, butter, extra-virgin olive oil, salt, pepper.

Put the thinly-sliced onion in a casserole with oil and a piece of butter. Sauté, and as soon as the onion begins to turn golden, add the peas. Season with salt and pepper and moisten with a little stock or hot water. Simmer slowly, and when the peas are nearly cooked add the diced ham and the chopped parsley. As a variation, cooked ham can be used instead of the raw Parma ham. The peas prepared in this way can also be used as a sauce for tagliatelle.

TOMATOES AU GRATIN

◀ *Umbria* ▶

4 ripe firm tomatoes, 1 handful parsley, 2 cloves garlic, black olive paste, breadcrumbs, extra-virgin olive oil, salt, chilli pepper.

Wash the tomatoes, cut in half and remove the seeds. Sprinkle the insides with salt and place them upside down on a sloping surface to let the water

set them on a rack to dry in the sunlight. Leave them out in the sun for about a week, bringing them inside at night so that they don't get damp. Finally place them in a jar and cover them with oil seasoned with garlic and chilli pepper. Close the jar, and wait at least 15 days before eating.

drain off. Chop the garlic and parsley very fine and mix with a few spoons of olive paste and a good dose of breadcrumbs. Moisten the stuffing with a little oil and season with salt and a pinch of chilli pepper. Arrange the tomatoes on an oiled ovenproof dish and fill with the stuffing. Sprinkle breadcrumbs over the top and a trickle of oil. Cook in a moderate oven for about half an hour, then turn up the heat to brown the top for about 10 minutes. If you wish, you may enrich the stuffing with capers or salted anchovies, and decorate with green or black olives. Served with boiled brown rice, this dish makes an excellent meal.

DRIED TOMATOES IN OIL

◀ *Puglia* ▶

Small tomatoes, garlic, extra-virgin olive oil, chilli pepper, salt, pepper.

Choose small, firm tomatoes. Clean them, cut them in half, sprinkle them with salt and lightly with pepper, and

PUNTARELLE

◀ *Lazio* ▶

Puntarelle *(chicory sprouts), 1 lemon, 1-2 cloves garlic, 2-3 salted anchovy fillets, extra-virgin olive oil.*

Remove the tougher outer leaves of the chicory heads (which you can use for soup) and chop the tender inner leaves. Scrape the roots, without cutting them off, quarter the heads and plunge them into

cold water mixed with a little lemon juice. Remove the salt and bones from the anchovies, chop them and mix them with the chopped garlic. Blend this mixture into a sauce with the olive oil. Drain the chicory, and place it in a salad bowl rubbed with garlic. Dress with the sauce and serve.

VEGETABLE PIE

◄ *Marche* ►

700 g potatoes, 1 onion, 3 big peppers (2 yellow, 1 red), 400 g ripe tomatoes, oregano, extra-virgin olive oil, salt, pepper.

Clean wash and slice all the vegetables, keeping them separate. Place them in alternate layers in an oiled ovenproof dish, seasoning each layer with oil, salt, pepper and oregano. Cook in a hot oven for about an hour, then remove and leave to cool for a few minutes before serving.

STUFFED ZUCCHINI

◄ *Marche* ►

8 medium-size zucchini, 300 g minced beef, 1 egg, 1 onion, 1 celery stalk, 1 carrot, parsley, grated nutmeg, grated Parmesan cheese, butter, salt, freshly ground pepper.

Top and tail the zucchini, slice them lengthwise and remove the inner flesh.

Chop the flesh as well as the onion, celery and carrot finely, and sauté in a knob of butter. Add the minced meat, season with salt, and cook for about fifteen minutes. Leave to cool, then mix with the egg, the grated parmesan, the chopped parsley, a pinch of nutmeg, salt, and freshly ground pepper. Stuff the zucchini with this filling, then set them in a frying-pan with a little butter and half a glass of water. Cook slowly for about 40 minutes, then serve.

ZUCCHINI ALLA SCAPECE

◄ *Campania* ►

1 kg zucchini, 4 cloves garlic, 1 bunch herbs (oregano, mint, bay leaves), 1 glass vinegar, 1 glass oil, salt, chilli powder.

Top and tail and wash the zucchini, then slice them in disks a few millimetres thick. Bring the vinegar to the boil with the bunch of herbs and a little salt, and reduce the liquid by about a third. Heat the oil in a frying-pan and fry the zucchini slices a few at a time.

Drain them, and lay them in layers in a pyrex or ceramic dish, seasoning with the sliced garlic, salt, chilli powder and the aromatic vinegar. Cover the container with clingfilm and leave in a cool place for 4-5 hours.

SWEETMEATS AND LIQUEURS

Rum Babà

◀ Campania ▶

For the babà dough: 300 g flour, 10 g butter, 5 eggs, 1 lemon, 1 cup warm milk, 1 dessertspoon sugar, 25g fresh yeast, salt.
Coating: 300 g sugar, 1 glass rum, apricot jam, 1 lemon.

Prepare the babà dough: cut the softened butter into pieces, cream it with the sugar and add the beaten eggs. Gradually add the flour, along with a pinch of salt, and last of all the grated lemon peel and the fresh yeast dissolved in warm milk. Mix thoroughly, then knead until you have a well-blended, elastic dough which doesn't stick to the sides of the bowl. Cover the bowl with a cloth, and leave to rise in a warm place. In the meantime butter the babà moulds, and sprinkle them with flour. After about an hour, knead the dough again for a few minutes, then fill the moulds. Cover them with a cloth and leave to rise again until they have doubled in size. Bake in a hot oven for about half an hour.

Meanwhile, prepare the dip: melt the sugar over the heat in 5 dl of water with a strip of lemon peel, until you have a smooth syrup. Take it off the heat and add the rum. Coat the babàs in plenty of syrup

while they are still hot. Finally heat the apricot jam with a little water and spread over the babàs.

Beccute

◀ Marche ▶

600 g flour, 100 g pine-nuts, 100 g walnuts, 80 g blanched almonds, 100 g raisins, 100 g dried figs, 100 g sugar, extra-virgin olive oil, salt.

Steep the raisins and the dried figs separately in warm water. Chop the walnuts and the almonds roughly. Put the flour, 4 dessertspoons of oil, the sugar, a pinch of salt, the drained and chopped figs, the well-squeezed raisins, the pine-nuts, walnuts and almonds into a large bowl and mix thoroughly. Gradually add warm water until you have a soft, smooth dough. Shape into tiny loaves, and line them up on a baking tray. Oil lightly and bake in a moderate oven for half an hour.

Bonet

◀ Valle d'Aosta-Piedmont ▶

8 eggs, 1 litre milk, 3 dessertspoons cocoa powder, 7 macaroons, 250 g sugar, 1 dessertspoon Marsala, 1 lemon.

In a bowl, beat the egg yolks with eight dessertspoons of sugar. Add the cocoa, the stiffly-beaten egg whites, and the lemon peel mixed with the crushed macaroons and the Marsala. Put the remaining sugar into a pudding mould with a hole in the middle, caramelise it, then pour in the mixture.

Cook the pudding in a bain-marie in the oven at minimum temperature for about three hours, with the bain-marie water just simmering. Test the pudding with a skewer; if this comes out dry, then it is cooked. Leave to cool, then put in the fridge for at least 4 hours before turning out of the mould to serve.

VALLE D'AOSTA COFFEE

◀ *Valle d'Aosta-Piedmont* ▶

1 4-person espresso machine of coffee, 2 small glasses grappa, 1/2 glass full-bodied red wine, lemon peel, sugar.

Make the coffee, then pour it into a saucepan and add all the other ingredients. Heat well, and serve boiling in the typical Val d'Aosta grolla, a wooden cup with several spouts. Place a lighted match close to each spout, producing a bluish flame. Then blow them out, and drink.

If you don't have a grolla, place the saucepan with all the ingredients on a small burner in the centre of the table, and heat it up, stirring all the time. When it is boiling, set alight, then take ladlefuls and pour them back into the pot from a height, so that the coffee flames as it descends. Dip the edges of the cups in sugar, and serve.

CANNOLI

◀ *Sicily* ▶

250 g ricotta cheese, 200 g flour, 150 g icing sugar, 50 g candied orange and lime peel, 30g dark chocolate, 20 g butter, 1 dessertspoon sugar, 1 teaspoon unsweetened cocoa powder, 1 teaspoon coffee powder, dry white wine, 1 egg, olive oil, salt.

To make the Sicilian cannoli you will need the special metal cylinders used for rolling the pastry round. These can be bought in shops selling specialised kitchen utensils.

Mix 150 g of flour, the cocoa powder, the coffee powder, the sugar and a pinch of salt in a large bowl, or in the centre of a floured board. Make a well in the middle and add the softened butter cut into small pieces. Knead thoroughly, adding as much white wine as necessary, until you have a smooth, soft, elastic dough. Roll the pastry up in a clean tea-cloth, and leave for about an hour in a cool, dark place.

Meanwhile prepare the filling: Place in a bowl the ricotta, sugar, finely-chopped candied peel, and roughly-grated chocolate. Mix well, then put in the fridge. Roll out the pastry a few millimetres thick, and cut out

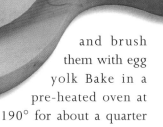

circles of about 10 cm. Stretch these to a more oval shape with your fingers, then roll them round the oiled metal cylinders, pressing down where the edges meet, and using a little egg white if necessary to seal them. Heat the oil in a high-sided saucepan, and fry the cannoli until they are evenly golden all over. Drain, and set to dry on absorbent paper. After a few minutes, remove the metal cylinders, and repeat the operation until all the pastry has been used up.

When the cannoli are cool, fill them with the ricotta cream and serve dusted with icing sugar.

CANTUCCINI

◄ Tuscany ►

300 g flour, 200 g sugar, 100 g almonds, 2 whole eggs and 1 yolk, 1 teaspoon grated orange peel, 1 teaspoon aniseed, 3 g bicarbonate of soda, butter, salt.

Sieve the flour and the bicarbonate into a bowl or onto a floured board and gradually mix in the sugar, a pinch of salt, the grated orange peel (without the pith), the aniseed and the unblanched almonds. Break in two eggs, and mix thoroughly, adding a little milk if the mixture is too dry.

Form three flat sausage shapes about an inch wide, lay them on a baking-tray and brush them with egg yolk Bake in a pre-heated oven at 190° for about a quarter of an hour, then cut into diagonal slices to obtain the classic cantuccini shape, and return to the oven for a further five minutes.

SICILIAN CASSATA

◄ Sicily ►

For the sponge: 150 g flour, 150 g sugar, 25 g butter, 5 eggs, salt.

For the filling and decoration: 500 g ricotta cheese, 300 g mixed candied peel, 250 g sugar, 200 g apricot jam, 100 g dark chocolate, 2 dessertspoons shelled pistachios, 1 small glass Maraschino, 1 small glass orange-flower water, 1 vanilla pod.

Prepare the sponge cake: dissolve the sugar in the egg yolks, and beat thoroughly with a wooden spoon until you have a soft cream. Gradually add the flour, continuing to stir well for 15 minutes. Add the butter melted in a bain-marie, and the salt. Beat the egg whites stiffly, and gently fold them in spoonful by spoonful. Pour the mixture into a tin (traditionally, a rectangular tin is used) and bake in a hot oven for half an hour, until the cake

comes away from the sides easily. Once it has cooled, cut into slices about 1 cm thick and use these to line a rectangular or round mould, previously lined with greaseproof or oiled paper. Warm the apricot jam over the heat, and dilute with the orange-flower water, then spread this over the inside of the sponge.

In a small saucepan, dissolve the sugar in half a glass of water with the vanilla pod, stirring until it takes on the consistency of a syrup. Leave to cool, remove the vanilla-pod, and mix with the ricotta, beating well with a wooden spoon until you have a smooth, lump-free cream. Add the diced candied peel and the chocolate chopped into small pieces, the shelled pistachios (plunge in boiling water, and dry thoroughly) and the *Maraschino*. Pour the ricotta mixture into the mould, banging it down on a work-surface to remove any air-pockets from the mixture.

Put in the fridge and cool for at least two hours. Turn the cake out very carefully, and glaze it with the apricot jam and orange-flower water mixture. Return to the fridge to cool before serving.

CASTAGNACCIO

◀ *Tuscany* ▶ 📷

300 g chestnut flour, 50 g raisins, 30 g pine-nuts, extra-virgin olive oil, salt.

Set the raisins to steep in warm water, and in the meantime blend the chestnut flour with water until you have a

soft, thick paste. Add the pine-nuts, the squeezed-out raisins and a pinch of salt. Mix well and then stir in a few dessertspoons of extra-virgin olive oil. Oil a baking-tin and sprinkle it with breadcrumbs, then pour in the mixture and bake in a moderate oven for about 40 minutes. The castagnaccio is ready when the top has formed a dark crust tending to crack.

Variations on the traditional recipe include the addition of a diced apple, fennel seeds, carob flour, or rosemary etc.

CELLUCCI

◀ *Abruzzo-Molise* ▶

600 g flour, 250 g sugar, 250 g grape conserve, 5 eggs, 1 stick vanilla, 1 lemon, 2 packets baking powder, 1/2 small glass milk, 1/2 glass extra-virgin olive oil.

In a bowl, beat the sugar, eggs and oil very hard until you have a smooth, thick, frothy mixture. Heat the milk with 2-3 pieces of lemon peel and the vanilla stick, then leave to

cool, and strain. When the milk is at room temperature, dissolve the baking-powder in it and fold it gradually in to the egg and sugar mixture. Mixing all the time, add the flour a spoon at a time, making sure that you blend it in perfectly. The dough should be fairly stiff, but manageable.

Break off pieces about the size of a mandarin and, with a floured rolling-pin, roll them out to a sole fillet shape about 1/2 centimetre thick. Put a spoon of grape conserve in the centre of each one, then roll the pastry up and place on an oiled baking-tray, shaping into the form of a celluccio, or little bird. Leave enough space between the pastries for them to rise during baking. Place in a moderate oven and remove when they have turned a nice golden colour. Pass a brush moistened in water over each pastry, and sprinkle with caster sugar.

ALMOND CRESCENTS

◀ *Liguria* ▶ 📷

250 g almonds, 200 g icing sugar, 3 eggs, 2 dessertspoons distilled orange-flower water.

Plunge the almonds in boiling water for a minute, peel them, and roast them in the oven for about 10 minutes. Slice about ten of them finely and put aside. Let the others cool, chop them and pound them in a mortar with the sugar until you have a fine paste. Mix this with the eggs and continue blending, adding enough orange-flower water, to produce the consistency of a dense purée. Put this into

a piping-bag and pipe crescent shapes onto an oiled baking-tray. Sprinkle the sliced almonds over the crescents, and bake in a hot oven, making sure that the almonds on top do not burn.

BOLOGNESE RING

◀ *Emilia Romagna* ▶

400 g flour, 150 g sugar, 100 g milk, 80 g butter, 2 whole eggs and 1 yolk, 20 g baking powder, granulated sugar, salt.

Mix together the flour, sugar, baking powder and a pinch of salt, and pile in the middle of a floured board. Make a well in the centre and add the softened butter in small pieces, and two eggs. Without over-kneading, blend the ingredients into a soft smooth dough, then shape this into a ring on a buttered baking-tray sprinkled with flour. Make a few oblique cuts in the top of the ring, and brush it with egg yolk and sprinkle with granulated sugar. Bake in a moderate oven for about half an hour, until the top has turned golden.

Among the numerous variations on this famous recipe, we recommend the addition of a teaspoon of grappa to the cake mixture.

CICERCHIATA

◀ Puglia ▶

500 g flour, 500 g honey, 4 eggs, 200 g extra-virgin olive oil, almonds, powdered cinnamon, sugar, chocolate flakes, olive oil, salt.

Prepare a soft dough by blending the flour, eggs, oil, 4 dessertspoons of sugar and a pinch of salt, making sure that the oil is evenly absorbed by the flour. Divide the pastry, and roll it into long sausage shapes, then cut these into pieces about 1 cm long. Shape them like gnocchi, by pressing them lightly over the back of a grater. Fry in boiling oil until they are golden. Heat the honey separately in a small saucepan until it turns a fine amber colour. Dip the fried sweetmeats into the honey, and when they are well-coated, place them in a ring-shape on a large serving-dish. Decorate with flakes of toasted almond and chocolate, cinnamon powder and sugar.

136

FRUSTINGOLO

◀ Marche ▶

200 g (generous) flour, 1 kg dried figs, 400 g raisins, 1 kg walnuts, 500 g almonds, 100 g dark chocolate, 200 g sugar, 1 glass extra-virgin olive oil.

Steep the washed figs and raisins in warm water, and shell the walnuts and the almonds.
Chop the chocolate, figs, walnuts and almonds into pieces, then mix all the ingredients together in a bowl, blending thoroughly. Spread the mixture in an oiled baking-tin, and bake for an hour.

GALÀNI

◀ Veneto ▶ 📷

300 g flour, 2 eggs, 2 oranges, 50 g butter, icing sugar, olive oil, salt.

Put the eggs, flour and the juice of the 2 oranges in a bowl, and mix thoroughly. Stir in the butter melted in a bain-marie, and a pinch of salt, and blend. Roll out the pastry quite thin, and cut out fairly large square or lozenge shapes (about 4x10 cm). Fry in boiling oil until golden, drain, and leave to dry on absorbent paper. Dust with plenty of icing sugar before serving.

BILBERRY GRAPPA

◀ Trentino Alto Adige ▶

1 kg black bilberries, 1 litre grappa, 2 kg sugar.

Mix the ingredients together, crushing the bilberries thoroughly, then place in a glass container. Leave in the sunlight for 40 days, shaking the contents frequently. Then filter, and bottle. This grappa is best served cold.

GUBANA

◀ *Friuli Venezia Giulia* ▶

For the pastry: 600 g flour, 450 g sugar, 100 g full-cream milk, 90 g butter, 4 egg yolks and 1 white, 1 lemon, 1 measure rum, 15 g fresh yeast, salt.
For the filling: 250 g shelled walnuts, 250 g shelled, blanched almonds, 250 g sultanas, 150 g pine-nuts, 100 g sugar, 300 g cocoa powder, 1 measure rum, 1 measure grappa, grated nutmeg, 1/2 teaspoon cinnamon powder, butter.
For the glaze: 1 egg, sugar.

Prepare a leavening base by dissolving the yeast in warm milk and mixing it with 3 dessertspoons of flour. Leave to rise in a warm, dark place, then add the butter melted in a bain-marie. After this, incorporate the sugar, a pinch of salt, the grated lemon peel, the remainder of the flour, 2 egg yolks and 1 stiffly-beaten white. Knead the pastry at length, adding a little milk or water if the dough seems too stiff, then leave to rise in a warm, dark place.
In the meantime, prepare the filling: chop the walnuts, almonds and pine-nuts finely. Wash the sultanas, steep them in grappa for a while, then chop. Heat the cinnamon powder in a small saucepan with a little butter. In a bowl, combine all these ingredients with the cocoa powder, sugar, rum, grappa and a pinch of grated nutmeg.

Knock down the pastry, adding the remaining two egg yolks and the measure of rum, and knead thoroughly to a smooth, even dough. Dust a tea-cloth with flour and roll the pastry out to a thickness of a few millimetres. Spread the filling on top, along with a few flakes of butter, then roll it up like a swiss-roll with the help of the tea-cloth. Place on a baking tray (preferably lined with greaseproof paper) arranging the roll in the typical spiral shape of the gubana. Cover with a tea-cloth, and leave to rise for a while in a warm place. Then brush the surface of the pastry with beaten egg, and cook in a pre-heated oven (180° C) for about 40 minutes. Serve dusted with sugar.

LIMONCELLO

◀ *Campania* ▶

400 g sugar, 5 dl 95° alcohol, juice of 1 lemon, the peel of 6 lemons, 16 lemon leaves.

Set the lemon leaves and peel to macerate in the alcohol in a hermetically-sealed jar in a dark place for 15 days, shaking the jar from time to time. When the time is up, add 5 dl of water mixed with the lemon

juice and sugar, and leave aside for 24 hours. Filter carefully, bottle, and leave to rest for a month.

MARITOZZI

◀ Lazio ▶

250 g flour, 2 dessertspoons sugar, 50 g raisins, 30 g pine-nuts, 30 g candied orange and lime peel, 25 g fresh yeast, 2 dessertspoons olive oil, salt.

Dilute the yeast in warm water, and mix it with sufficient flour to make a firm dough. Cut a cross in the top, place it in a bowl covered with a tea-cloth, and leave to rise in a dark place for 3 hours. Adding the oil, and as much water as required, mix the leavening dough with the rest of the flour, 2 dessert-spoons of sugar and a pinch of salt. Knead well, then add the pine-nuts, the raisins − previously steeped in warm water, then squeezed − and the roughly chopped candied peel. The dough should be well-blended and fairly soft.

Shape the dough into small oval rolls, and place them on an oiled baking-tray, leaving enough space between for them to rise. Cover with a tea-cloth and leave to rise in a warm place for at least 4 hours.

Pre-heat the oven to 180°-200° C and bake the maritozzi until they turn an even, golden colour. Note: When cooked, they should be soft and not crusty.

MYRTLE LIQUEUR

◀ Sardinia ▶

600 g ripe myrtle berries, 1 litre 90° alcohol, 2 litres water, 500 g sugar or 600 g honey.

Clean the berries with a rough cloth. Place them in a container of dark glass with the alcohol, and leave them to infuse for 15 days. When the time is up, strain, filter, and press the berries to re-lease the rich flavour. Add a cold sugar syrup made from 2 litres of water and the sugar (or honey) and pour into dark-glass bottles.

139

NEPITELLE

◀ Calabria ▶

350 g flour, 3 eggs, 100 g ricotta cheese, 100 g raisins, 50 g lard, 30 g sugar, 30 g icing sugar, 1/2 a lemon, 1/2 an orange, 1 dessertspoon brandy, salt.

In a bowl, mash the ricotta with a fork, then blend it with a dessertspoon of sugar using a wooden spoon. When you have a smooth cream add the chopped raisins, the grated lemon and orange peel and the brandy, and mix thoroughly.

Beat two eggs with the remaining sugar. Place the flour in the middle of a work surface, and pour the egg mixture into a well in the centre. Blend the ingredients, then knead the dough thoroughly by hand for about half an hour. Divide the pastry in half, then roll it out with a rolling-pin into two thin sheets. Brush these with an egg which has been beaten with a dessertspoon of water. On one sheet place little piles of filling about 3 cm. apart. Place the other sheet of pastry on top, then press your fingertips down in the empty spaces to stick the two sheets together. Roll a pastry wheel along the unfilled spaces to cut out the little filled squares, then lay them out on a baking-tray and sprinkle with lard.

Cook in a pre-heated moderate oven (200° C) for about 40 minutes. Remove when the nepitelle are golden, and serve dusted with icing sugar.

Saint John's Walnut Liqueur

◀ *Emilia Romagna* ▶ 📷

500 g sugar, 350 g 95° alcohol, 19 fairly small green walnuts, 4 cloves, 2 g cinnamon, peel of 3 lemons.

On the feast of St. John the Baptist (24 June) collect the walnuts, cut them into four, put them in a jar with the alcohol, and then close it tightly. The next day, add the other spices, and leave to macerate until 3 August, shaking the

jar well three times a day. Then filter, and add the sugar dissolved in 300 g of hot, but not boiling water.

Leave to cool, bottle, and wait at least three months before consumption.

Variations on the preparation of this liqueur include the addition of other spices, such as mace, rose petals, etc.

Pandoro

◀ *Veneto* ▶

500 g flour, 200 g sugar, 200 g butter, 40 g fresh yeast, 2 whole eggs and 3 yolks, vanilla.

The recipe for the famous Verona pandoro is a secret well-guarded by the industrial manufacturers of this legendary cake. The recipe provided here will enable you to produce, possibly not "the real thing", but a home-made pandora which is certainly not without its merits.

In a large bowl, blend the yeast, 90 g of flour, an egg yolk and 10 g sugar into a soft dough. Cover with a clean cloth, and leave to rise in a warm place for 3-4 hours. Then mix together 150 g of flour, 30 g of butter melted in a bain-marie, 70 g of sugar and 2 egg yolks, and add them to the first dough. Knead the mixture thoroughly by hand until it is perfectly blended, then leave to rise again for a couple of hours. At this stage, incorporate the remaining flour, 50 g sugar, 30 g butter melted in a bain-marie and two whole eggs, kneading the dough again energetically, and then leave to rise for a further two hours. When the time is up, knock the dough down, and work in a pinch

of vanilla.
Roll it out flat,
and dot the surface
with the remaining
butter in flakes. Fold
the edges of the
dough in to the centre
to form a packet, then
roll out again and repeat
this operation twice. Then leave to
rest for half an hour, and roll out and
fold once again. Finally, form the
dough into a ball, and place it in a
mould dusted with sugar, leaving it to
rise in a warm place. When the dough
has risen to the edges of the mould, set
it to bake in a moderate oven for about
45 minutes, lowering the heat after the
first 15 minutes.

142

PANETTONE

◀ *Lombardy* ▶ 📷

700 g flour, 250 g sugar, 225 g butter, 200 g raisins, 70 g candied lime and orange peel, 6 egg yolks, 2 lemons, 20 g fresh yeast, 10 g salt, almonds to decorate.

Prepare the leavening base: dissolve the
yeast in a few dessertspoons of warm
water, add 100 g flour, and enough
water to form a firm dough. Shape into
a ball, cut a cross on the top and set in
a covered bowl to rise in a warm place
for about half an hour.
Place half the remaining flour in a
large bowl, and incorporate the leavened dough and enough water to re-
produce the previous consistency.
Knead well, and leave to rise again in a
well-floured, covered bowl in a warm

place until it
has doubled
in size. Knock
down the
dough,
knead-
ing it
well, and
add the remaining
flour, the butter melted in a
bain-marie, the sugar dissolved
in the egg yolks, a pinch of salt and the
grated lemon peel. If necessary, add a
little warm water, and knead thoroughly until you have a soft, shiny
dough. Steep the raisins in warm water, then dry them and dust with flour,
and dice the candied peel. Blend these
well into the dough. Line a suitable
cake tin (round and high-sided) with
greaseproof or buttered paper, and set
the dough inside. Cut a cross in the
top, and sprinkle with a few blanched
almonds, pressing them lightly into
the dough. Pre-heat the oven to 200°
C, and bake for 10 minutes, then turn
down the heat to 170° C and continue
cooking for a further 30-40 minutes.

PANNA COTTA

◀ *Valle d'Aosta-Piedmont* ▶

500 g cream, 200 g icing sugar, 100 g sugar, 50 g milk, 2.5 sheets icinglass (or gelatine) 1/2 vanilla pod.

In a saucepan, heat the cream with the
vanilla pod and the icing sugar (you
can pulverise granulated sugar in an
electric mixer) and stir until the sugar
has dissolved, making sure that the

mixture doesn't boil, then take off the heat.

Dissolve the isinglass or gelatine in two dessertspoons of milk, and add to the cream. Put the sugar into individual moulds, or one large one, and caramelise it, then pour in the cream. Place in the fridge to cool for a few hours, then turn out the mould(s) and serve. A variation can be made without caramelising the sugar, serving the cooked cream instead with a raspberry sauce.

PANPEPATO
(SPICEBREAD)

◀ *Umbria* ▶

350 g flour, 250 g honey, 125 g almonds, 125 g sugar, 2 eggs, 1 small lemon, 6 dl oil, 1/2 packet baking powder, allspice, 1 clove, salt, pepper.

Melt the honey, sugar and oil in a saucepan, stirring carefully.

Mix the flour with the baking powder, a pinch of pepper, the powdered clove, two pinches of allspice (a peppery spice, for this reason also known as Jamaica pepper), and a pinch of salt.

Blend the ingredients, incorporating the eggs one at a time, then the honey syrup, and the grated lemon peel.

Leave the mixture to rest in a covered bowl for a while, before shaping and baking in the oven.

The mixture can be baked either as one large cake, or a number of small buns. Once cool, it can be covered with plain or chocolate-flavoured glacé icing.

144

PAPPAI BIANCU

◀ *Sardinia* ▶

100 g cornflour, 1 litre milk, 200 g sugar, 1 lemon.

This pudding was traditionally made with starch extracted from the wheat after lengthy maceration. Now it can simply be bought.

In an earthenware pot, blend the cornflour with a little cold milk, then pour over the rest of the milk and the sugar, and cook over a moderate heat, stirring all the time with a wooden spoon. When the milk begins to thicken add the washed and dried lemon peel.

Finally, pour the mixture into a moistened pudding-basin, or small individual moulds, and leave to cool before serving.

PAPPASINOS

◀ *Sardinia* ▶

1 kg white flour, 500 g shelled almonds and walnuts, 500 g raisins, 500 g sugar, 400 g lard, 50 g dark, bitter chocolate, 5 eggs, 2 oranges, 1 lemon, aniseed, 1 piece cinnamon bark, 1/2 packet vanilla, 2 packets baking powder, butter.

Plunge the walnuts in boiling water for a few minutes, and toast the almonds in the oven to remove the peel from both. Chop half roughly, and put the rest in a mortar and grind to a paste. Wash the raisins, and leave them to steep in a little warm water. In the meantime, beat the eggs and the sugar vigorously in a bowl for about fifteen minutes until they are smooth and frothy. Fold in the almonds and walnuts, aniseed, grated cinnamon and the drained and dried raisins.

Melt the lard in a bain-marie, cool and fold into the mixture, blending in thoroughly. Add the vanilla, the grated orange and lemon peel, and the chocolate, previously melted over a low heat. Then gradually fold in the flour and the baking powder, and stir slowly with a wooden spoon until the dough is evenly mixed.

Turn the dough onto a floured board, and knead lightly by hand. Then roll it out to a thickness of about 1 cm, and cut into lozenge shapes. Place these on a baking-tray, and bake in a very moderate oven for about 20 minutes.

PASTIERA NAPOLETANA

◀ Campania ▶

For the pastry: 200 g wheat flour, 100 g sugar, 100 g butter, 1 whole egg and 1 yolk, salt.
For the filling: 500 g ricotta cheese, 200 g sugar, 200 g wheat (pre-cooked or left to steep in water for a few days) 50 g icing sugar, 40 g candied lime, 40 g candied orange, 30 g butter, 5 eggs, 2 dl milk, 1 lemon, cinnamon, salt.

Prepare the shortcrust pastry: place the flour mixed with the sugar on a floured work surface, and put into a well in the centre the softened butter cut into small pieces, a whole egg and one yolk and a pinch of salt. Knead the ingredients together, working rapidly, until you have a soft, smooth dough, then cover with a cloth and leave in a cool place for half an hour.

In a saucepan cook the wheat with the milk, butter and the grated peel of half a lemon for about ten minutes, stirring all the time. Blend together the ricotta, sugar, the rest of the grated lemon peel, a pinch of cinnamon and one of salt. Mix thoroughly until you have a smooth cream, then add the roughly-chopped candied peel. At this stage, incorporate the yolks of 4 eggs and the wheat mixture and finally fold in 3 stiffly-beaten egg whites. Roll out two-thirds of the shortcrust pastry about half a centimetre thick and line an oiled and floured cake-tin. Pour in the filling, and turn the edges in over it. Cut strips about half a centimetre wide from the remaining pastry, and arrange these over the tart to form a grid pattern. Brush with beaten egg, and bake in a moderate oven for about an hour, Serve dusted with icing sugar.

145

PIZZELLE

◀ Abruzzo-Molise ▶

600 g flour, 250 g sugar, 5 eggs, 1 stick vanilla, 1 lemon, 1 packet baking powder, 1/2 glass milk, 1/4 litre extra-virgin olive oil.

This traditional cake from Abruzzo has to be cooked using a special iron utensil. Nowadays this is usually electric, while it the past it was heated by being placed among the coals in the fireplace.

Put the sugar, eggs, and oil into a large bowl and beat vigorously until they are soft and creamy. Heat the milk with 2-3 pieces of lemon peel and the vanilla stick, leave to cool and then filter. Put the baking powder into a cup, and dissolve it in the milk, which should be at room temperature, then fold it gradually into the egg and sugar mixture. Continue stirring slowly, and incorporate the flour one spoonful at a time, blending it in well to produce a soft batter. Heat the electric iron and grease both sides (traditionally pork fat was used). Place a spoonful of the batter on the iron, close, and cook the pizzelle until golden.

RICCIARELLI

◀ *Tuscany* ▶ 📷

250 g icing sugar, 150 g shelled sweet almonds, 15 g bitter almonds, 1 egg, 20 wafers.

Blanch the almonds by plunging them in boiling water, then dry them off in a hot oven. When they are cool, grind them by hand or in a mixer, and mix them with the icing sugar (keeping a little aside). Beat the egg whites stiffly, then delicately fold in the almond paste one spoon at a time. When the mixture becomes too stiff to stir, turn it onto a work-surface dusted with icing sugar and knead by hand. When you have a smooth paste, roll it out with a rolling-pin about 1 1/2 cm thick, and cut out disks the same size as the wafers. Lay the wafers out on a baking-tray, and place a disk of almond paste on each. Cover with a tea-cloth and leave for about an hour in a cool place. Then bake in a moderate oven (without letting the biscuits brown) for about half an hour. Cool, trim off any excess wafer, and serve dusted with icing sugar.

CANDIED PEEL

◀ *Sicily* ▶

1 kg citrus fruits, 750 g sugar.

Procure oranges, lemons, grapefruit, and, if possible untreated limes.
Wash carefully, dry and cut in strips about 1 cm wide, leaving some fruit attached to the peel.
Proceed with each of the fruits separately as follows. Boil in water for about 15 minutes, then place in a large frying-pan with a third less than the weight of the fruit in sugar: a kilo of fruit requires about 750g of sugar.
Caramelise the fruit over a lively heat, making sure the sugar does not burn.
Remove from the heat when the sugar syrup coating the fruit has the right consistency and has turned a golden colour.
Cool on a marble slab, then roll in sugar. Preserve in a hermetically-sealed jar.

SBRISOLONA

◀ *Lombardy* ▶ 📷

200 g wheatmeal flour, 200 g cornflour, 200 g almonds, 150 g sugar, 120 g butter, 100 g lard, 2 egg yolks, 1 lemon, icing sugar, vanilla flavouring, salt.

◆ Blanch the almonds by plunging them in boiling water, then dry and chop them.

◆ Mix the two types of flour and pile them in the middle of a floured work-surface. Make a well in the centre, adding the sugar, chopped almonds, egg yolks, grated lemon peel, a pinch of salt and one of vanilla flavouring.

◆ Rub in the ingredients thoroughly, then make another well in the centre and add the softened butter and lard cut into small pieces. Knead all the ingredients well together. You won't achieve a compact dough, but what is important is that the ingredients are well-blended.

◆ Grease and flour a cake-tin, and press the dough into it in an even layer. Before putting it into the oven, beat the tin down on the work-surface to remove any air-pockets. Bake in a hot oven for about an hour, leave to cool, then serve dusted with icing sugar.

HONEY *SEBADAS*

◀ *Sardinia* ▶ 📷

600 g flour, 400 g fresh Sardinian pecorino cheese, 6 eggs, bitter honey, 80 g lard, oil for frying.

Pile the flour in the middle of a floured board, then put the eggs and the lard in a well in the centre and mix and knead thoroughly until you have a smooth, even pastry. Roll it out very thin, and cut into squares. Place a piece of pecorino in the centre of each square, and fold up the edges, pressing them together well. Fry the sebadas in plenty of oil in a frying-pan, then place them on absorbent paper, dip them in a little bitter honey, and serve hot.

SFOGLIATINE

◀ *Veneto* ▶

350 g flour, 200 g butter, 1/4 litre milk, 20 g baking powder, 4-5 dessertspoons sugar, 1 egg yolk, salt.

Mix together the flour, sugar, milk, baking powder and a pinch of salt. Gradually incorporate the butter, blending it in thoroughly. Roll out the pastry on a floured surface, and leave it to dry out for about twenty minutes. Then cut out small rectangles, and brush them with egg yolk, and with a

syrup made by heating the sugar with a little water. Lay the pastries on a buttered baking-tray, and bake until golden.

APPLE *STRUDEL*

◀ *Trentino Alto Adige* ▶

<u>For the pastry</u>: *250 g flour, 1 egg, 2 dessertspoons oil, salt.*
<u>For the filing</u>: *2 kg apples, 150 g breadcrumbs, 250 g butter, 80 g sugar, 50 g raisins, 50 g pine-nuts, cinnamon, lemon.*

On a floured work-surface, mix the flour with the egg, oil and a pinch of salt with one hand, while with the other you add water drop by drop until you have the right consistency. Knead to a smooth and elastic dough, then shape it into a ball, grease lightly, and leave to rest in a cool, dark place for half an hour.

Meanwhile, peel and core the apples, and slice them finely, and lightly roast the breadcrumbs in 150 g of butter. On a well-floured tea-cloth, using both your hands and the rolling-pin, roll out the pastry as fine as you can without letting it break. Melt the remaining butter, and brush it over the pastry. Leaving a space at one end, spread the filling over it: first the breadcrumbs, then the layer of sliced apples sprinkled with sugar, followed by the steeped and squeezed raisins, the lightly toasted pine-nuts and the grated lemon peel. With the help of the tea-cloth, roll up the strudel very carefully starting from the filled end. Then place it on a greased baking-tray,

and brush with the melted butter. Bake in a hot oven for about half an hour and serve warm, dusted with icing sugar.

CHOCOLATE CHESTNUT TRUFFLES

◀ *Liguria* ▶

400 g chestnuts, 75 g sugar, 1 cup milk, 1 measure liqueur, 1 dessertspoon cocoa powder, 1 square dark chocolate, vanilla, salt.

Peel the chestnuts and cook them in salted milk for about 40 minutes. Then drain them and put them through a food-mill. Mix the sugar with the chestnut purée, then dry it out on the heat.
Leave to cool, then add the liqueur and the cocoa powder, and blend thoroughly. Form into balls the size of a walnut, roll in cocoa powder and serve.

TORCOLO

◀ *Umbria* ▶

400 g flour, 200 g sugar, 150 g pine-nuts, 50 g candied peel, 50 g raisins, 1 egg, 10 g bicarbonate of soda, 1 pinch aniseed, 60 g butter, salt.

Dice the candied peel, chop the raisins, and toast the pine-nuts in the oven for about 3 minutes then pound them in a mortar. Pour the flour onto a floured work-surface, and place in a well in the middle the softened butter, the pine-nuts, sugar, bicarbonate and aniseed, the egg and a pinch of salt. Rub in all the ingredients, knead thoroughly for a few minutes, then add the raisins and the candied peel. Shape the dough into a ring, and place it on a buttered and lightly floured baking-tray. Bake in a pre-heated oven at 200° C for about half an hour, until the top turns golden. Leave to cool before serving.

BUCKWHEAT CAKE

◀ *Trentino Alto Adige* ▶

250 g buckwheat flour, 250 g sugar, 250 g blanched almonds, 250 g butter, 6 eggs, 1 packet vanilla-flavoured sugar, 500 g red bilberry jam, icing sugar, salt.

Soften the butter at room temperature, cut it into pieces and cream with 150g sugar. Incorporate the egg yolks one at a time, blending to a smooth, soft consistency. Gradually stir in the buckwheat flour, a pinch of salt, the chopped almonds, and the vanilla-flavoured sugar. Beat the egg whites stiffly, fold in the remaining sugar, then incorporate this into the cake mixture. Pour into a buttered and floured cake-tin, and bake in a pre-heated oven at 180°C for about an hour. Remove from the oven and leave to cool. Split the cake, spread with the bilberry jam, and dust the top with icing sugar.

POTATO AND RICOTTA CHEESE TART

◀ Friuli Venezia Giulia ▶

450 g potatoes, 80 g flour, 60 g sugar, 2 teaspoons baking powder, 1 egg, 1 lemon, 80 g butter.

For the filling: 350 g fresh ricotta cheese, 60 g icing sugar, 1 whole egg and 2 yolks, 20 g butter.

Boil the potatoes, then peel and mash them. Put the mashed potato in a bowl, and incorporate the flour, the butter melted in a bain-marie, the egg, baking powder and the grated lemon peel. Blend thoroughly until smooth, then line a buttered flan-tin with the potato pastry.

Prepare the filling by mashing the ricotta with a fork, then blend in one whole egg and two yolks, the icing sugar, and the butter melted in a bain-marie. Stir well until smooth and creamy, then spread on the pastry base and bake in a pre-heated oven (180°-200° C) for about half an hour.

RICOTTA TART

◀ Campania ▶

300 g flour, 200 g ricotta, 100 g pine-nuts, 100 g raisins, 1 egg, 1 lemon, vanilla, 2 dessertspoons honey, 80 g butter, 1 dessertspoon extra-virgin olive oil, salt.

Rub the butter into the flour, then add a pinch of salt, 1 dessertspoon of honey and enough water to mix to a smooth dough. Leave the pastry in the fridge for about half an hour. In the meantime prepare the

filling. Place in a bowl the ricotta, the raisins (previously washed and steeped in warm water) 50g pine-nuts, half a dessertspoon of honey and a little grated vanilla. Add about a glass of water, and beat vigorously to a thick cream. Put the remaining pine-nuts, the egg, the other half-spoon of honey, the oil and the grated lemon peel in a dish, mix thoroughly, and add to the ricotta mixture. Butter a flan-tin and sprinkle it with flour, then roll out the pastry and line it, leaving the pastry higher than the rim. Fill with the ricotta mixture, and bake in a moderate oven for about an hour. Serve cold.

TAGLIATELLE TART

◀ Emilia Romagna ▶

For the shortcrust pastry: 300 g wheat flour, 120 g sugar, 80 g butter, 2 egg yolks.
For the tagliatelle: wheat flour as required, 1 egg.
For the filling: 100 g sugar, 100 g butter, 120 g shelled sweet almonds, 15 g shelled bitter almonds, 50 g chocolate powder, 1 measure Sassolino wine, juice of 1/2 a lemon.
For the decoration: 20 g butter, 20 g candied lime peel, icing sugar.

153

Prepare the shortcrust pastry using the above ingredients. Mix the flour and sugar and place in the centre of a floured work-surface. Make a well in the centre and add the softened butter cut into small pieces and the egg yolks. Rub in rapidly, and knead until you have a soft, smooth dough. Roll the pastry into a ball, and leave in a cool place covered with a cloth for about half an hour.

To make the tagliatelle, mix the egg with enough flour to produce a stiff dough, then knead thoroughly and roll out thinly and leave to dry out for a while. After this, roll it up and cut into thin strips, then open these out and lay them on the floured work-surface. Now prepare the filling. Plunge the sweet almonds in boiling water, peel, and toast them lightly in the oven. Then chop them finely and mix with the butter, sugar, the chopped bitter almonds, the chocolate, the Sassolino and the lemon juice. Roll out the pastry on a floured work-surface with a rolling-pin, and line a flan-tin, keeping the edges slightly higher than the rim. Pour in the filling, level the surface with a knife, then turn the edges of the pastry in over the filling. Cover the surface of the tart with the tagliatelle, sprinkle with melted butter, and lay a piece of buttered paper lightly over it. Bake in a moderate oven (180°C) for about half an hour. Take the tart out of the oven, remove the paper, then sprinkle the surface with the finely-chopped candied lime and dust with icing sugar. Leave in a cool place for 24 hours before serving.

CARNIVAL *TORTELLI*

◄ *Lombardy* ►

250 g flour, 70 g butter, 4 eggs, 1 lemon, olive oil, salt, icing sugar.

In a tall saucepan, bring 3 dl of water to the boil, adding the butter cut into pieces, the salt and grated lemon peel. Sprinkle in the flour, beating carefully with a whisk to avoid lumps forming.

Continue blending vigorously over the heat until the mixture gathers off the sides of the pan to form a firm ball. Remove from the heat and add the sugar, then leave to cool before adding the eggs one by one. Continue to blend thoroughly until the dough is smooth and shiny.

Heat the oil in a frying-pan, then drop in spoonfuls of the dough. Allow the tortelli to swell, fry them golden on both sides, then leave to dry on absorbent paper. Serve dusted with icing sugar.

VIN COTTO

◄ *Puglia* ►

Good quality ripe grapes.

In the cuisine of Puglia "cooked wine" is used instead of honey to sweeten cakes; it is very easy to make. Choose the best bunches of grapes, remove from the stalks and sieve finely. Filter the resulting juice to remove any impurities, then pour it into a container (earthenware is best, never aluminium) and cook, stirring all the time, over a very low heat until it thickens to the consistency of runny honey. Pour into sterilised, hermetically-sealed containers, and store out of direct sunlight.

ZABAIONE

◄ *Valle d'Aosta-Piedmont* ►

10 egg yolks, 300 g sugar, 1/2 litre dry Marsala.

This famous cream is traditionally made with dry Marsala, but this can be

substituted with other wines such as Madeira, Sherry, Port, dry white wine or even champagne. The procedure is the same, but the resulting flavours are quite different.

In a bowl, beat the egg yolks with the sugar using either a whisk or a wooden spoon until they are white and frothy. Stir in the Marsala, and place to cook over a slow heat (preferably in a bain-marie), stirring constantly with a wooden spoon. The cream will increase in volume and thicken; remove from the heat before it boils. The zabaione can be served with biscuits or used as a cake-filling.

ZALETTI

◀ Veneto ▶ 📷

250 g maize flour, 100 g cornflour, 330 g raisins, 250 g sugar, 6 eggs, 1 litre milk, 100 g butter, 2 lemons, 1 vanilla pod, salt.
For the custard: 4 egg yolks, 80 g sugar, 2 dessertspoons flour, 1/2 litre milk, 1 lemon.

Bring the milk to the boil with a pinch of salt and the vanilla pod, then remove the pod, and sprinkle in the two mixed, sieved flours. Mix thoroughly, then remove from the heat and stir in the sugar and the butter. When all the ingredients are thoroughly blended, leave the dough to rest for a couple of hours.

In the meantime prepare the confectioner's custard. In a tall saucepan, mix the egg yolks with the sugar, and once the sugar has dissolved, gradually stir in the flour. Stirring constantly, add the boiling milk and the grated lemon peel. Put the saucepan on the heat and bring to the boil, stirring all the time. When it has boiled for three minutes, remove from the heat and leave to cool. Take the dough and incorporate the eggs, one at a time, the grated lemon peel, the cooled confectioner's custard, and the raisins - steeped in warm water, drained, dried and lightly floured. Blend thoroughly, then shape the dough into small circles about 5cm in diameter, and not too thin, and lay them on a buttered baking-tray. Bake in a hot oven for about half an hour. Serve warm, dusted with icing sugar.

ZELTEN

◀ Trentino Alto Adige ▶

200 g flour, 100 g dried figs, 100 g shelled walnuts and hazelnuts, 50 g raisins, 50 g pine-nuts, 50 g candied orange peel, 60 g butter, 20 g fresh yeast, 1 egg, 2 cups milk, 2 dessertspoons honey, vanilla, peeled hazelnuts and almonds to decorate, salt.

Steep the raisins and the chopped figs in warm water. Mix the flour with a pinch of salt and place in a large bowl. Make a well in the centre, and add the yeast dissolved in a little warm water and a teaspoon of honey. Blend the yeast with a little of the flour to make a leavening base, and leave to rise for about half an hour. After this, add to the flour the softened butter cut into small pieces, the remaining honey and the egg. Knead the dough well, adding a little milk if necessary, until it is smooth and soft. Now add the drained and squeezed figs and raisins, the pine-nuts, the chopped walnuts and

hazelnuts, and the roughly chopped candied orange peel. When all is well blended, cover and leave to rise for a couple of hours in a warm place, away from draughts. Butter a round cake-tin and sprinkle it with flour, then place the dough inside. Decorate the top with a few almonds (blanched in boiling water, then dried) and walnuts. Bake in a hot oven for about an hour. The zelten should not be eaten straight away, and is best kept for at least 36 hours. Well-covered and stored in a cool place, it keeps for a long time.

ST. JOSEPH'S ZEPPOLE

◀ Campania ▶

500 g flour, 15 g fresh yeast, 100 g sugar, 1 egg, 1 lemon, milk, 50 g butter, olive oil, icing sugar.

Dissolve the yeast in a little warm water, stir well, then add a little flour and knead into a soft dough. Leave this to rise for half an hour, then add the egg, a little warm milk, the sugar, the butter melted in a bain-marie, the grated lemon peel and the rest of the flour. Mix well, then knead thoroughly until you have a smooth, firm dough. Break off small pieces, shape them into rings, then leave them to rise on a floured tea-cloth. Fry in boiling oil, remove the zeppole when they are golden, and lay them to dry on absorbent paper. Serve dusted with icing sugar.

INDEX

STARTERS

Aubergine starter 8
Bagna caûda 8
Bruschetta 9
Cazzilli 10
Cecina 10
Crab with lemon...........................15
Crescia 12
Crostini alla ciociara 13
Crostini with chicken livers............13
Crostini with truffle 12
Crostini with "liptauer" 13
Dressed olives 16
Erbazzone...............................13
Fettunta 14
Fiadone 14
Fried olives 18
Green anchovies 8
Mozzarella in carrozza 16
Nervetti................................15
Olive all'ascolana 16
Panzanella 18
Pasqualina (Easter) pie 22
Pilchards in *saór*.......................20
Pugliese *bruschetta*.....................9
Red chicory in *saór*.....................19
Rice croquettes 19
Sage biscuits.............................9
Salami in vinegar 19
Scallops au gratin 10
Seafood salad 15
Stuffed mussels...........................10
Sweet-savoury pie.........................21
Tomato *panzerotti* 18
Vol-au-vent mushrooms 24

FOCACCIA, BREAD, PIZZA, SAVOURY PIES

Calzone 28
Calzone with vegetables 28
Carasau bread or "music sheet" bread...29
Chicory pizza 33
Country pizza with onion 34
Crescenta 29
Focaccia with oil.......................29
Frattau bread 30
Neapolitan pizza 33
Piadina romagnola 32
Potato pizza 32

Pugliese bread 30
Sfinciuni...............................35
Tarallucci 35
Tuscan bread 32

SAUCES

Meat sauce with aromatic vinegar....38
Peará sauce 39
Sea urchin sauce..........................38
Sorrentina sauce..........................38

FIRST COURSES

Acqua Cotta 42
Agnolotti of Friuli 44
Baked lasagne.............................52
Baked *pizzoccheri* 61
Barley soup...............................84
Broad bean and chicory soup 83
Bucatini all'amatriciana 45
Bucatini ammudicati 45
Bucatini with lamb sauce 45
Canederli 45
Cappelletti in broth 46
Casoncelli..............................46
Cavatieddi with rocket 47
Celery soup...............................84
Cheese and pepper spaghetti...............72
Chickpea soup 82
Ciuppin 48
Fish soup 44
Fusilli with broad beans 49
Gnocchi alla valdostana 49
Goulash soup 83
Jota 50
Macaroni timbale 77
Macaroni with
ricotta and sausage.....................54
Maize soup 83
Malloreddus 54
Mille cosedde 54
Minestra maritata.......................54
Neapolitan *agnolotti* 42
Orecchiette with broccoli 55
Pancotto 56
Pansotti with nuts......................57
Pappardelle with hare sauce.............57
Pasta alla Norma 57
Pasta and beans 58
Pasta with chickpeas......................58
Penne all'arrabbiata 60

158

Pici with rabbit 60
Potato *culingionis* 48
Potato *gnocchi* 50
Pumpkin *tortellini* 78
Quadretti in broth
with chicken livers 62
Ribollita 62
Rice *sartù* 66
Rice with pork chops 64
Riso all'isolana 62
Risotto pilòta 68
Risotto with mushrooms 64
Risotto with saffron........................64
Sagne chine 65
Sardinian *minestrone* 55
Scripelle 'mbusse 66
Spaghetti *alla carbonara* 72
Spaghetti *alla chitarra*
with meat sauce 70
Spaghetti and tomato 70
Spaghetti with bottarga 74
Spaghetti with clams........................74
Spaghetti with cuttlefish ink 70
Spaghetti with garlic,
oil and chilli 67
Spaghetti with pilchards 74
Spaghetti with wild asparagus 67
Spicy meat soup 84
Strangolapreti 74
Tagliatelle with black truffle...........76
Tagliatelle with bolognese
meat sauce 76
Tortellini in broth 77
Trenette with *pesto* 80
Trofie 80
Truffle agnolotti (ravioli) 42
Vincisgrassi.......................................82

MEAT DISHES

Braised oxtail 90
Chicken in spicy sauce 100
Cinghiale alla cacciatora 90
Cotechino 91
Escalopes in balsamic vinegar........101
Falsomagro.......................................92
Finanziera 92
Florentine beefsteak 87
Fondue 94
Goulash 95
Horsemeat *pastissàda* 97

Lamb in *potacchio* 86
Lepre alla cacciatora 95
Liver, Venetian style 92
Mixed boiled meat 87
Mixed fry, Piedmont style 94
Mutton stew 102
Pheasant with
mushrooms and onions 92
Pigeons in *salmì* 98
Polenta pasticciata...........................98
Polenta taragna 100
Pot roast with Barolo 88
Puccia 100
Rabbit in *porchetta*..........................91
Roast kid 89
Roast lamb
with "mentuccia" mint 86
Roast *pajata* 96
Roast piglet......................................96
Roast rabbit 90
Roast shin of pork 101
Roast spring lamb with potatoes 86
Saltimbocca alla Romana 101
Scottiglia 101
Stewed lamb.....................................97
Stewed venison 89
Stuffed breast of veal 89
Stuffed pigeons................................98
Sweet and sour hare 95
Uccellini scappati 102
Veal shanks, Milanese style 96
Vitello tonnato
(Braised veal with tuna mayonnaise) 102

159

FISH DISHES

Baccalà alla Livornese
(Livorno-style salt cod) 106
Baccalà alla Vicentina
(Vicenza-style salt cod) 106
Cacciucco (Livorno fish soup) 108
Lake whitefish in foil 112
Panada asseminese.........................112
Pike in sauce..................................110
Sardines *a beccaficu* 113
Scampi alla busara 113
Stuffed squid 108
Swordfish *agghiotta* 106
Tuna, Catania style........................113
Whitefish with
tomatoes and potatoes 112

VEGETABLE DISHES

Artichokes *alla giudia* 116
Asparagus with Parmesan cheese ..116
Baked aubergines 121
Baked *lampascioni*
(wild onions) 121
Beans in the flask 118
Broad beans *alla scafata*................120
Caponata
(Sicilian style ratatouille) 116
Cardoons *alla brindisina* 117
Chickpea meal fritters....................120
Dried tomatoes in oil......................125
Fried artichokes 117
Orange salad 120
Peas with Parma ham.....................124
Peperonata......................................122
Peppers with breadcrumbs 124
Potato pankake................................122
Puntarelle.......................................125
Sauerkraut 118
Stuffed aubergines 122
Stuffed zucchini 126
Sweet and sour onions 117
Tomatoes au gratin.........................124
Vegetable pie 126
Zucchini *in capece* 126

SWEETMEATS AND LIQUEURS

Almond crescents 134
Apple strudel 150
Beccute..128
Bilberry grappa 136
Bolognese ring 135
Bonet 128
Buckwheat cake 152
Candied peel...................................146

Cannoli 129
Cantuccini 130
Carnival *tortelli* 154
Castagnaccio 132
Cellucci 132
Chocolate chestnut truffles 152
Cicerchiata.................................136
Frustingolo 136
Galàni 136
Gubana 138
Honey *sebadas* 150
Limoncello 138
Maritozzi 139
Myrtle liqueur.............................139
Nepitelle 139
Pandoro 140
Panettone 142
Panna cotta 142
Panpepato 144
Pappai biancu 144
Pappasinos 144
Pastiera Napoletana....................145
Pizzelle 145
Potato and *ricotta* cheese tart 153
Ricciarelli 146
Ricotta tart 153
Rum *babà* 128
Saint John's walnut liqueur...........140
Sbrisolona 148
Sfogliatine 150
Sicilian *cassata*........................130
St. Joseph's *zeppole*...................156
Tagliatelle tart 153
Torcolo 152
Valle d'Aosta coffee.....................129
Vin cotto 154
Zabaione 154
Zaletti.......................................155
Zelten 156